The ABCs of Autism Acceptance

Sparrow Rose Jones

Owned by disabled workers, Autonomous Press
seeks to revolutionize academic access.

Autonomous Press is an independent publisher focusing on works about disability, neurodivergence, and the various ways they can intersect with other aspects of identity and lived experience.

ISBN-10: 0-9972971-7-4

ISBN-13: 978-0-9972971-7-1

Cover art, "Autistic Abecedarian," is by the author, Sparrow Rose Jones. Sparrow's art is therapeutic, expressive, and political. Find more of Sparrow's writing, music, and art at **http://www.sparrowrose.com**

Table of Contents

Acknowledgements

While writing is most often a solitary venture, creating a book requires a community. I would like to especially thank:

those who contributed to the GoFundMe campaign that paid for the solar electricity that fueled writing and editing of this and future books:

Bridget Allen; Elizabeth Bartmess; Colin Bowman; Andrew Dell'Antonio and the whole Dellakawa household; Karla Fisher; Alex Forshaw; Stephanie Kuipers; Shalia Martin; Caitlin McGuren; Colleen and Alex Rosebaum; Jeanie Schmidt; Sean Roycroft; Stimtastic.co stim toys, chewable jewelry and fidgets for autistic adults and teens (and kids too!); Charla T-H; P.D. Workman; Cathy Wright; and four anonymous donors– you know who you are. Thank you so much.

I would also like to thank those who hosted me in their homes as I wrote certain chapters:

Sharon DaVanport; Larry Hopkins; Wayne and Carolyn Jones; Beth Ryan and Scott Jacobson; Chris and Jennifer Brown.

Paul Erdös is known for saying that a mathematician is a machine for turning coffee into theorems. In that same spirit, I happily turn coffee into books and would like to thank the wonderful local coffee houses where certain chapters found their first form:

CoHo in Pocatello, Idaho; Giddy-Up Coffee & Kitchen in Bellevue, Idaho; The Coffee Grinder in Ketchum, Idaho; Spic and Span Laundry and Coffee in Laramie, Wyoming; Pony Espresso in St. Joseph, Missouri; Mojoe's Coffee Bar in Glasgow, Kentucky.

I also want to thank the editing and publishing crew at Autonomous Press, especially my co-editors, Michael S. Monje Jr. and Nick Walker. I also need to say thank-you to:

Carolyn Ogburn, for going above and beyond in helping me promote

the ideas in this book,

and the entire Autistic community, for emotional support, collegial discussions, and the tireless daily activism that strives to re-shape this world into a place that not only tolerates difference, but lovingly accepts it.

Introduction

This book began its life as a self-challenge. April is a difficult month for me because Autism Speaks has declared it to be "autism awareness month," which means a month of turning off my car radio because I can't handle the degrading advertisements being played. It means a month of seeing Autism Speaks donation tins in restaurants and coffee shops and having to choose between spending my precious and unpredictable energy on educating the shop owners or quietly leaving and secretly fuming at myself for not saying anything. It means a month of signs announcing charity walks to benefit a charity that drains money from local organizations and doesn't give back to the people it promises to help. April is a month of hearing what a tragic burden on families and society people like me are. And then, after a month of being buffeted by all the messages of awareness, most of the world goes back to quiet ignorance for another eleven months. During the only time of the year most people care about us, the world is filled with negative and inaccurate statements about us.

You see, I am an Autistic adult, so all those messages of despair are about me and people like me. I hear the terrible things that are said about autism and those of us who are Autistic and I have to wonder if the people saying those things believe we don't have feelings. Or maybe they think we're too far gone to ever hear what they're saying about us. But they are wrong. We hear and understand and hurt. And not just Autistic adults, but children too. We hear what is said about us, and it is devastating.

So I wanted to challenge myself to counter all that with messages of acceptance. My goal was to write something every day in April (with one day off per week), working my way through the alphabet as I talked about ways to understand and accept us better. As you can see, I made it through the alphabet, though only about half of these alphabet essays were actually written in the month of April. The end result of that self-challenge is this book, filled with ups and downs, joys and frustrations. This is a book about ways that it is wonderful to be Autistic and ways that the world makes it very difficult for us Autistics to find a place to survive and thrive in it. As I wrote, sometimes I felt myself speaking to fellow Autistic adults, and at other times to parents of Autistic children. I've tried to keep things accessible so anyone can find their way through these words, even if they've never been close to Autistic people or the activist movements we tend to gravitate toward, such as the social justice movement and the neurodiversity movement. I wanted this to be a book that was accessible to everyone because autism acceptance only works when we get as many people as possible on board with these important ideas: presume competence, do not try to fix us for we are not broken, help us to live the fullest and most fulfilling lives we can, always remember to include us as the main stakeholders in the decisions that are made about us and our future. There is a classic slogan in the larger disability community: nothing about us without us. We are so often sidelined to be spectators in our own stories. As a result, the Autistic community has embraced this slogan as well. We want to be an active part of the decision-making process. We want to be center-stage in our own lives. It is our right.

If you are outside the borders of the U.S. and reading this book, you may feel it is heavily U.S.-centric. Sadly, you would not be wrong in that assessment. I have tried to write from a more universal perspective, but the truth is that I have lived in the United States all my life. Here is where I have experienced my Autistic life and here is where I have come into contact with legislation activism, oppression, and more. I apologize to my siblings in other countries for being so focused on the details of my own country, but I can only write what I know. I beg all of you to please write about your Autistic lives in your countries, so I can read all of you and learn more about the rest of this wide, wonderful world. I also beg your forgiveness for the parochial poverty of my own limited experiences, from which I write. Please know that my words may not speak of you but my heart does reach out to you in hopes of solidarity all the same. I do not know your world but I value all of you and look forward to your words.

Bring an open mind to this book. You may feel challenged by some of what you read. Some of these essays will make you angry or sad. I hope all of them will move you to action. I want you to challenge ableism. I want you to listen to Autistic people. I want you to help us as we work to make the world a better, safer place for us to live. If you are Autistic, I want you to love and accept yourself for who you are at this moment, and to never give up on yourself in your quest to be the person you dream of being. You will always be Autistic, and that is a wonderful thing. Embrace who you are and work to become the best you can be. The world needs your voice– whether it comes from your mouth, your hands, or someplace else entirely. The world needs your opinions and dreams. But also know that your value does not lie in how useful you are to the world. The world does need you, but that is not what makes you a worthwhile and precious human being. You have inherent value because you are you. There was never a person like you in this world before and there will never be another identical to you again. This is your time on this earth and I want you to always remember that you belong here and that you are a vital piece of the great mystery.

A is for Acceptance

You may have noticed in the last half-decade or so that there is a growing trend toward speaking of autism acceptance instead of autism awareness. Autism awareness, in and of itself, is not inherently bad. By now, most people are aware that there is "a thing called autism" but, in my experience, most people are not very aware of what "that autism thing" actually is. So I do, at least partially, agree with the people who say we still need more awareness.

What I have a problem with is the form that awareness tends to take.

A week before the month of April even began, I had to stop listening to the radio because all the stations were already gearing up for April with lots of "awareness" and lots of advertisements about awareness events. I heard a lot about "children with autism" and nothing at all about Autistic adults. Not only do we age out of most services when we turn 18, but we also become invisible. It's as if the entire world stops caring about us once we are no longer cute children to worry about and, instead, just inconvenient adults to be stuck with.

I heard a lot of scare talk, including hearing autism repeatedly compared to diabetes, cancer and AIDS. Diabetes, cancer and AIDS kill children. Autism does not. Diabetes, cancer and AIDS are illnesses laid on top of a child's underlying identity– they can change a child's philosophy, but they do not change innate aspects of their identity. Autism is a cognitive and perceptual difference that is so deeply rooted in our neurology that it cannot be separated from our identity. Beneath cancer, there is a healthy child hoping to break free of disease. Beneath autism, there is more autism– it's autism all the way to the core. Autistic children do not "go into remission," we develop coping skills and we mature into Autistic adults, and we work to learn ways to communicate with those around us.

There might be suffering that can be alleviated– seizures brought under control, gastrointestinal disorders treated, methods learned and sometimes medications taken for mitigating anxiety or other difficulties– but this suffering is not autism. Like many other genetically-based human variants, autism tends to come along with a higher rate of certain conditions. While these conditions (such as epilepsy, gastroparesis, Ehlers-Danlös syndrome, or circadian rhythm disorders) occur more frequently alongside autism, it is crucial to remember that they are not autism. It is also important to remember that Autistic adults quite often do not resemble the Autistic children they once were– we grow and develop all our lives– but Autistic adults are still every bit as Autistic as when we were children, no matter how many coping skills are learned, no matter how "indistinguishable from our peers" we might seem to have become.

At the center of the autism awareness movement is an organization known as Autism Speaks that functions like a giant magnet, drawing all donations to them. In the ten years that Autism Speaks has been around, local organizations have watched their funding dry up. Autism Speaks dominates the autism charity scene now and, as a result, they have the power to set the tone when it comes to "awareness." The tone the organization has chosen to set is one of despair and misery. We are portrayed as burdens who break up marriages and destroy the lives of those around us. We have been compared to "lepers" (an outdated term for people with Hansen's Disease) and our parents are compared to saints for taking care of us. The awareness that is being put forth is shaped around a rhetoric of fear. Autism Speaks is one of the few organizations that is widely hated by the population it was established to serve. As one of the organization's very few token autistic board members, John Elder Robison, said when he resigned, "No one says the Cancer Society does not speak for them. No one describes the Cystic Fibrosis Foundation as an evil organization.   All that and more is said of Autism Speaks every day.   I've tried to be a voice of moderation but it hasn't worked. Too many of the views expressed by the organization are not my own; indeed I hold very different points of view."

So that is autism awareness. That is what we are rejecting. Of course we want people to be aware of autism, we just don't want the awareness brought by groups like Autism Speaks. We do not want a dishonest awareness that diminishes us. We are only seeking the sort of awareness that leads to understanding and acceptance. Often, I hear people rejecting the notion of autism acceptance because they are mistaken about what it actually is. They think it means giving up and doing nothing to make a person's life better.

They think of it as sinking beneath the waves and drowning. They mock those who support acceptance, accusing us of believing that life with autism or with an Autistic family member is nothing but "unicorns and rainbows all the time." They hate the idea of autism acceptance because they don't understand what it is.

Autism acceptance is seeing us as whole, complete human beings worthy of respect. Autism acceptance is recognizing that we are different and helping us learn to work within our individual patterns of strengths and weaknesses to become the best people we can be, not trying to transform us into someone we are not. Autism acceptance is remembering always that Autistic people are listening, including those who might appear not to be, and choosing to speak of autism and Autistic people in ways that presume competence and communicate value.

> "Tolerance says, 'Well, I have to put up with you.' Awareness says, 'I know you have a problem and are working earnestly to fix it.' Acceptance says, 'You are amazing because you are you, and not despite your differences, but because of them.'" – Kassiane Sibley, Autistic author and blogger at *Radical Neurodivergence Speaking*.

> "Acceptance is about recognizing that an autistic person is, and will always be, different but not less – even as some challenges are addressed." – Amy Sequenzia, Autistic poet and blogger at *Non-Speaking Autistic Speaking*.

> "Autistic people are not viewed as able beings, this view makes us suffer." – Emma Zurcher-Long, Autistic blogger at *Emma's Hope Book*.

> "Autism Acceptance means supporting the Autistic person in learning the things they want to learn and in gaining the skills they need for what they want to do. Autism Acceptance is the radical assertion that at the level of broad, overarching principles, what Autistic people need isn't that different. We need to be accepted for who we are. We need to hear that we're OK, we need to hear that the things we have trouble with don't make us broken or lazy or horrible people. We need people's actions towards us to reflect that. We need

people to listen when we say we need help, and we need people to listen when we say we don't. We need to be taken as the whole people that we are, and we need to be met with the understanding that we are the experts in our own lives and abilities." – Alyssa Hillary, Autistic author and blogger at *Yes, That Too*.

"Good teaching is based in deep respect for the individual, the cognitive learning style of each student, the shared excitement about the topic of study. Best practice in teaching autistic students isn't any different, though these faculty would be insulted if I told them so." – Carolyn Ogburn, writer and educator at TAG.

"Over the past two years, I have asked Tyler many times how he feels about having autism. And while he clearly understands how the autism negatively affects his social skills and attention, he always tells me that he likes his autism. Although he has also told me, at times, that he wants to be 'normal,' he continues to insist that his autism helps him. So if he likes his autism, do I really have the right to counsel him otherwise?" – Kymberly Grosso, mother of an Autistic son and *Psychology Today* blogger at *Autism in Real Life*.

"If you have the autism acceptance song in your heart, add Paula [C. Durbin-Westby] and Estée [Klar]'s voices to your blog rolls, Subscribe to their blogs. Tweet, 'like', and show your respect and support to these powerful women. Don't allow their names to fade into internet oblivion as others try to opt into autism acceptance because it is now the fashion. They were doing it before it was cool. It is easier to say accept autism now because others paid the high cost for daring to say it before us." – Kerima Çevik, mother of an Autistic son and blogger at *The Autism Wars*.

"Acceptance means accepting yourself as you are, even in the face of persistent attempts throughout your life to get you to be what you are not. Especially in the face of persistent attempts throughout your life to get you to be what you are not. The best you can be is Autistic. Let me explain. 'The best you can be is Autistic' means that you are at your best when you are being fully who you are, able to express yourself and move through the world in ways that are right for you, comfortable for your body. 'The best you can be is Autistic' does not imply impairments, 'less than,' 'can only do so much.' On the contrary, it means that you are who you are- your pervasive Autistic self (which actually includes those parts that observers might think are 'typical' just because they can't see anything that looks unusual to them), and that encompasses all of who you are, not just the parts that have been 'permitted,' and not just the stuff that whatever the DSM of the moment says are your deficits. You have the right, or should, to grow in ways that are good for you, that you think are good for you. You have the right to make changes in your life that you think are the correct ones for you." – Paula C. Durbin-Westby, Autistic blogger, musician, and founder of Autism Acceptance Day/Month/Year/Decade

This is, at minimum, a book about autism acceptance. What I hope it turns out to be for you, dear reader, is a book about autism understanding, welcoming, appreciation, support, and love. Acceptance is merely a starting point, a bare minimum. I challenge you to go farther than acceptance. I challenge you to welcome Autistic people into your life. I challenge you, Autistic people, to love who you are – at this moment and every moment in what the poet, Mary Oliver, calls "your one wild and precious life."

B is for Bullying

"All kids get bullied; it's a rite of passage!"

"Just ignore them and they will get bored and stop."

"They only bully you because they're jealous of you. Be bigger than them and ignore it."

"We can't coddle our kids. Bullying will toughen them up and make them ready for the world."

We see a lot of talk about bullying these days and we hear a lot of schools talk about their "zero tolerance" anti-bullying programs, but bullying is just as bad as ever and Autistic kids (and adults!) are particularly vulnerable. We get more than our share of bullying and we often have fewer resources to cope with bullying than other children do. (And, make no mistake, bullying hurts ALL children, regardless of neurology.)

CBS News[1] reported that 63% of Autistic children have been bullied and are three times more likely to be bullied than their siblings without autism. When I listen to the stories of the Autistic adults I know, it feels like that figure is too low. I told my parents about a lot of the bullying I faced in school, but there was a lot more I didn't tell them about. I was ashamed of the way I was treated. I felt like it did no good to tell, so why bother? My mother knew about the day I was boxed in the ear because the whole side of my head was still red when she saw me hours later. But I was too ashamed to tell her about the sexual lies about me that my classmates had published in the gossip column of the school newspaper. When I talked with her recently about the sexual slander, she didn't believe it could have happened because I was attending a high-quality private school at the time. "The school wouldn't have let that happen," she said. Sadly, she is wrong; it did happen, even there.

Mom knew about the defacement of my (very expensive) school yearbook because she wanted to see the yearbook when I brought it home. She was angry about what the other children had done to my book. I misunderstood her anger and thought she was angry at me for letting it happen (if you've ever been the subject of a nasty game of "keep away," you know there is no "letting" involved when fellow students destroy your property.) Because I misunderstood her anger, I was afraid to tell her about other incidents of bullying. This is why it is so important to let your children know that you don't blame them for the bullying they receive. If you don't make it clear that your anger is directed at the bullies, not at your child, you leave room for your child to assume the guilt themselves. Even worse, if you suggest your child is bringing the bullying on themselves, don't expect your child to feel safe continuing to tell you what is going on at school. If your child feels that you are blaming them, you have shut the door on communication between the two of you and that leaves your child even more vulnerable to being hurt by bullies.

---

1. CBS News URL: http://www.cbsnews.com/news/survey-finds-63-of-children-with-autism-bullied/

The survey reported in the CBS news article involved asking parents of Autistic children about bullying. Another report from Time Magazine[2] says Autistic students were bullied almost five times as much as non-autistic students, with a 46% rate of being bullied. Parents in this study said they felt the true rate was even higher than that and the actual incidence of bullying may be even higher still, because parents don't always know or even suspect many of the things that are happening at school. Their children may be afraid to reveal the bullying, too ashamed to talk about it, or even apathetic due to a belief that no one can help them anyway. This can also be due to depression caused by the bullying. Their children may have lower communication skills that don't provide those children with the tools to adequately communicate what is going on in school (and parents can be fooled about their children's communication skills because a large vocabulary and high verbosity can mask an inability to assimilate and communicate more complex emotional content). In many cases, the children may not even fully realize that they are being bullied. I think sometimes I missed realizing that I was bullied, and there are situations that I look back on as an adult and realize more of what was happening– situations where I thought the other children were my friends, but when I remember our interactions, I am shocked to realize that they were doing horrible things to me and that I kept coming back for more because I didn't know any better back then. I thought they were my friends because they were interested in me and paying attention to me.

The first time I remember being bullied was in second grade. I am pretty sure I must have been bullied earlier, especially considering what I remember of my behavior in first grade (I was an odd child). But the first I remember was when I was seven years old. Someone, I have no idea who, had heard me playing piano and asked if I could come to the office and play a piece over the intercom during morning announcements. I played a piece I loved, called "Whirling Leaves," that ran up and down the whole keyboard. I loved the sensation of crossing my hands over each other up and down the keyboard so that piece was my favorite to play.

When I was done and had returned to my classroom, a boy who sat near me said, "you finally did something right." It was what I have come to learn is

---

2. URL: http://healthland.time.com/2012/09/05/why-autistic-kids-make-easy-targets-for-school-bullies/

called a "back-handed compliment," and while I didn't know the name for a comment like that, it still stung and put a tarnish on my day. More than my day, apparently, since it still stings forty years later.

That is very mild bullying, though. As kids grow up, their bullying gets both more subtle and more overt. The psychological bullying gets more subtle, harder to counter, harder to get help with. The kids around me matured at a different rate and in different ways than I did, and I never had any idea how to deal with the bullying words. The bullying got more physical around middle school as well, and that physical bullying definitely got more and more overt over time.

For anyone who says bullying is just a rite of passage or harmless, they should pay attention to the ways Autistic pre-teens and teens get bullied. I was boxed in the ear, had rocks and bottles thrown at me, was hit in the head with a plank (science class, studying inertia and gravity with balls rolling down boards), had bleach thrown on my clothes, was tricked into eating a laxative chocolate bar . . . and other things enough worse that I don't feel like talking about them. My high school teachers had sworn to me that there would be no more bullying in university. They were wrong. I had fellow students grab my test paper to see my grade and then pretend they were going to punch me, fists stopping inches from my face, because I got an A and they didn't. A professor– a grown man in a position of power– would growl at me like a rabid dog when he passed me in the halls. I had been promised that university would be a haven for people like me but instead I was excluded and bullied, just like every other place I have gone to school or worked.

And all that I went through was mild compared to what other Autistic students have faced. In the autumn of 2014, an Autistic teen in Ohio was tricked by classmates who said they were doing the ice bucket challenge when instead they poured human waste on him, filmed it, and shared the video around school.[3] In January of 2015, an Irish teen had his pants and underwear pulled down and was forced to eat twigs while the bullies filmed the attack and later posted it on Facebook.[4] In March, 2015, an Autistic teen

---

3. URL: http://www.nbcnews.com/news/us-news/charges-filed-against-ohio-teens-sick-ice-bucket-prank-n225746

4. URL: http://www.irishexaminer.com/ireland/boy-14-with-special-needsforced-to-eat-twigs-321513.html

in Louisville, Kentucky was threatened by a classmate with a knife and then choked so hard by that same classmate that the teen was too injured to return to class.[5] In 2013, an Autistic teen in Australia had both hands blown off and shrapnel embedded in his legs, down to the bone, by bullies who gave him a bomb made from a golf ball.[6]

I could go on and on, because these stories are popping up all the time, every week. Sometimes every day. What's worse, often teachers and the parents of the bullies say the Autistic children deserved the bullying they got. Sadly, that doesn't surprise me– I got a lot of bullying from teachers in elementary, middle, and high school, too.

Parents of bullies in a recent incident in Iowa were reported in the media as claiming that the Autistic teen who their children were bullying had "brought it on himself." One specific example given was of the teen using insulting language toward a classmate, who then punched the teen in the face. I don't know what children are taught now, but I was brought up to believe that it is wrong to respond to words with blows. A relative of the teen who punched the Autistic teen for saying the wrong thing said they were proud of their nephew for punching the teen. Even the school principal and the president of the school board claimed no bullying was happening.

I'd like to know what happened before the Autistic teen called others names. I have a good guess. I used to get bullied and bullied and bullied until I couldn't take it any more and lashed out. Then I was blamed for everything that had happened, even though my behavior was a reaction, not a cause. Since I was not as subtle as my more mature classmates, I was always the one who got caught misbehaving. I was always the one blamed for bad behavior. Quite often, I got punished for defending myself while the bullies were treated as if they were the victims. I suggest that's most likely what was happening in the Iowa case as well.

Bullying is just another example of why we need to fight so hard for autism acceptance. Children take their cues from teachers and parents. Look

5. URL: http://www.wlky.com/news/mother-sues-after-autistic-son-is-allegedly-bullied-hurt-at-school/32134002

6. URL: http://www.theaustralian.com.au/news/ipswich-teen-loses-both-hands-after-thrown-a-homemade-bomb/story-e6frg6n6-1226639706999

at how the Iowa parents, and even the school principal, responded to the bullying situation– they said the Autistic teen deserved to be bullied. And the parents and principal were very aware that the teen was Autistic. Yes, we need awareness of autism but awareness alone is just not enough. Awareness left that young man out in the cold, blamed for the abuse others heaped on him. We often get blamed for how others treat us because we aren't always able to read the behavioral signs that tell people who and what to avoid, so we "walk right into it" and then get blamed by people who think we should have known better.

While it is very important to presume the competence of Autistic people, it's equally important to understand what sort of things– things that might seem simple or obvious to non-autistic people– are outside our range of control and perception. It's bad enough to get treated horribly by others, but to then get blamed for how we've been treated is outrageous. "Presume competence" means, as Dr. Douglas Biklen has explained,[7] "approach each child as wanting to be fully included, wanting acceptance and appreciation, wanting to learn, wanting to be heard, wanting to contribute." It doesn't mean to assume that a person faces no barriers, and it is never an excuse for withholding supports and accommodations. "Presume competence" most definitely is not a call for blaming disabled people for struggling with those barriers.

Imagine blaming a Blind student for not being able to read the chalkboard. Would parents and school blame a child who uses a wheelchair for not being able to attend classes on the second floor if there is no elevator in the building? So why is it that Autistic schoolchildren so often get blamed for the bullying they experience and get told that they are bringing the social punishment on themselves? The more articulate and academically able an Autistic child is, the more likely they are both to encounter bullying and to be blamed for it. We need concepts like "presume competence" to remind us that a person can have strengths in one area despite weaknesses in another

---

7. URL: http://www.unesco.org/new/en/media-services/single-
view/news/douglas_biklen_winner_of_unesco_kuwait_prize_begin_by_presuming_competence/
#.VzOcTvmDGko

and that we should always play to those strength and, when in doubt, assume those strengths are there when we choose how to interact with that person. A child might be excellent in mathematics or be able to recite the names of all the bones in the body, yet still be confused in social situations and make choices that seem foolish to onlookers who don't understand the thoughts and processes going on inside that child's head.

Acceptance means teaching kids that Autistic people do have feelings, that we do have empathy, even if we don't always express it in ways that non-autistic people are capable of understanding, that we do have value, and that we are full members of the human race, deserving of dignity and accommodation. Acceptance means teaching others that when we don't understand what is going on, the proper thing to do is to help us, not to bully us. Acceptance means teaching principals and teachers how to understand bullying dynamics so that they can see more of what is going on, not just the desperate reactions of a badly bullied child with fewer skills of social subterfuge than their "more socially sophisticated" tormentors. (I wonder why it is that the people who have more social skills are the bullies while the people who have fewer are the victims? Perhaps our idea of what "social skills" actually are is unhealthily skewed?)

All of us need to work together to build a bully-free world for everyone. We need to understand bullying and have compassion for all involved. Yes, that means the bullies, too. We cannot allow them to continue bullying others, but people become bullies from a place of pain and lack inside themselves and part of ending bullying is recognizing that pain and lack and helping the bullies become happier people, too.

Until Autistic people are accepted, bullying will continue and it will be justified by those who don't understand what's happening. People must work to understand autism, and they need to know that Autistic people are different from non-autistic people in significant ways. People must come to see that Autistic people are trying our best and meet us with love, understanding, and acceptance, helping to mentor us in the confusing social ways of the culture that surrounds us.

Until we have full autism acceptance, there will always be people who see our vulnerabilities and think we are extra "fun" to torment and there will always be people in positions of power who do not see the whole picture and say that we deserved the abuse and brought it on ourselves. When we can move from ignorance to awareness to acceptance, we can move from violence and bullying to understanding, friendship, and love. A world of autism acceptance is a world I am eager to work toward every day. Please, let's all work toward that beautiful goal.

C is for Color

This isn't about lighting it up blue or walking in red or toning it down taupe. Today I want to talk about People of Color and autism.

When the average person thinks about autism . . . well, wait. I think maybe the average person rarely thinks about autism at all. Maybe in April, a bit. But when the topic comes up, the average person thinks of someone famous– usually Temple Grandin– or someone fictional– usually Dustin Hoffman's "Rain Man"– or a little boy. A little white boy. A little white boy from a middle-class family. There are many layers of erasure here, but the thing I want to point out today is that all of those images of autism are white. The erasure of Autistic People of Color is so pervasive that, while writing this essay, I nearly forgot the famous Autistic artist, Stephen Wiltshire[8]. He is a brilliant artist and quite famous, yet, as a white person thinking about mainstream representations of autism, he didn't pop into my mind until hours after I had written most of this chapter.

When the face of autism is nearly exclusively a white face what happens to Autistic African-Americans, Autistic Asian-Americans, Autistic Native Americans, Autistic Latino-Americans– any Autistic People of Color? Those folks are under-diagnosed, under-served, under-valued, and under-protected. This is a problem for all communities of Color. I am white, but dear friends have made me aware of some of the difficulties they and their families face and I want to do what I can to raise awareness and understanding of autistic issues of People

8. Bio at Wikipedia. URL: https://en.wikipedia.org/wiki/Stephen_Wiltshire

of Color because I firmly believe that until all of us are valued, accepted, and honored, none of us are valued, accepted, or honored.

This is a difficult topic for me because I am white and thus I am afraid of talking over People of Color or marginalizing others by filtering their lives and experiences through my lens of white privilege. Cody Charles, a writer who is Black but non-Autistic, addresses that concern in his essay "10 Common Things Well-Intentioned Allies Do That Are Actually Counterproductive,"[9] saying that "your choosing not to speak up has either to do with the fear of your oppressed identity being pounced on or the presence of your privilege." That is so true for me. As an impoverished, feminine-presenting metagender, disabled person I am also oppressed, but as a white person it is difficult for me to see past so many layers of privilege I have been largely oblivious to for most of my life. I am afraid of saying the wrong thing, making things worse, or misrepresenting people, but the difficulty I feel is so small compared to the huge struggles People of Color face. I am selfish if I cling to my nervousness in the face of other people's oppression and even death.

Charles writes that "the courageous few are tasked alone with holding the integrity of inclusiveness in spaces." I need to be one of those courageous few. Actually, we need to expand the courage beyond the few. We must all find that courage inside us. We cannot talk about autism acceptance without ensuring that it is an acceptance for all of us, not just for middle-class people, not just for speaking Autistics, not just for the university educated, not just for cis-gendered, male, heterosexual Autistics, and not just for white Autistics. Autism acceptance is for all and can only be for all when we are courageous enough to take up the discussion of Color and how it intersects with autism. The words of Black Autistics can be difficult to find and writing or speaking from Autistic People of Color who are not Black is even more difficult to find. What I most want you to come away from this chapter with is a passionate devotion to seeking out the words of Autistic People of Color. As a white Autistic person, I can tell you something about these issues, but only the people who live these lives themselves can tell you what it's *really* like.

9. URL: http://everydayfeminism.com/2015/10/counterproductive-allyship/

I worried about writing this chapter. I worried about talking over the voices of those you should really be listening to on this topic. I worried about not understanding the topic well enough to give it its full due. I worried about getting things so wrong that my friends who are People of Color became angry with me. In the end, my worries are not what matters. I might say the wrong thing. I might not say the right things. But to not say anything at all would be the greatest error of all.

So what does it look like for multiple communities of people to be under-diagnosed, under-served, under-valued, and under-protected?

Autism in Black[10] reports that diagnosis rates are the same across races but Black and Latino children are diagnosed significantly later than white children. This is a problem, because the sooner parents, teachers, doctors, churches, families, communities understand that a child is Autistic, the sooner everyone can learn how to work with that child's patterns of strengths and weaknesses and help that child to excel in every way possible.

Diagnosis can also be more difficult for adult Autistic People of Color who slipped through the cracks as the system was adjusting diagnostic criteria when they were growing up. Because the face of autism is so overwhelmingly white, as adults, Autistic People of Color often get disregarded and detoured when they seek diagnosis and assistance.

When an Autistic child or adult goes undiagnosed, too often the people around that person unfairly blame them for their troubles and often compound those struggles unnecessarily. Without diagnosis, people are left without accommodations, without appropriate learning plans or career assistance, and without the crucial understanding that leads to acceptance of the individual, divergent neurotype and all.

When you combine disparities in health care access with the stereotypes of autism as a childhood condition of mainly white boys, it is obvious why Autistic children who are People of Color are under-diagnosed and diagnosed late and People of Color who are Autistic adults so often go without diagnosis and the assistance it can bring to their lives. It is vital for their health and well-being that we all work to change the tendency to automatically think of autism as a white condition and that we help all Autistic people get timely and accurate diagnoses and recognition of their neurotype with everything helpful and respectful that

---

10. URL: http://www.autisminblack.com/

goes along with that recognition and understanding.

They are also under-served: Too often, Autistics of Color who need services end up in jail or prison instead. Autistic children and adults are at greater risk of ending up in the criminal justice system than the general population. Sixty percent of American prisoners are People of Color (twice the percentage of People of Color found in the general population).[11] When you combine the higher risk of imprisonment of Autistic people with the higher risk of imprisonment of People of Color, it is clear that we are letting too many people who need services in the community end up getting under-served (and often physically and psychologically destroyed) in prison instead.

There is a vicious circle here, too, that depends on under-valuing their contributions. Autistic People of Color are not visible in the autism/Autistic community, so white people are less likely to notice that nearly all the organizations and spokespeople are white. Without a visible presence of People of Color in leadership, the stereotypes about white autism are reinforced. It is time for all of us to speak up about the absence of People of Color in leadership roles in our communities. Without a diversity of perspectives and without a diversity of voices being heard with respect to the diversity of needs, we are letting our Autistic brothers and sisters and their families down. Inclusion means everybody. Until everyone is well-represented and heard and valued, we are all losing out.

When young Autistic men are also People of Color, racism and ableism become deadly. Too often, the police use excessive force in dealing with Autistic Black or Latino men in stressful situations. You've heard of the "crimes" called "driving while Black" or "walking while Black?"   Add to those, "being Autistic while Black."

For just one example out of hundreds, *Brobrubel's Blog* has an entry, "Autism in Black and White,"[12] that compares how John Elder Robison's son, Jack, was treated for building and detonating explosives to how Neli Latson was treated for sitting in the grass, waiting for the library to open. Jack Robison, who is white, got the attention of the Bureau of Alcohol,

---

11. URL:https://www.americanprogress.org/issues/race/news/2012/03/13/11351/the-top-10-most-startling-facts-about-people-of-color-and-criminal-justice-in-the-united-states/
12. URL: http://brobrubel.com/2011/12/28/autism-in-black-and-white/

Tobacco, Firearms, and Explosives when he detonated his explosives, but all charges were dropped and Jack was recruited by the University of Massachusetts chemistry program. Neli Latson, who is Black, sat down on the grass in front of the library to wait for it to open, getting the attention of the local police who handled the encounter very poorly, resulting in a prolonged jail term for Neli.

As a white person, I know that my voice should not be a front voice for the issues of People of Color, but this is everyone's discussion. We should all be talking about this. We should all be asking where the People of Color are in our community. What is most important is that the voices we should be listening to on these issues are those of People of Color. The role of white allies is to encourage everyone to talk about these issues and then be quiet and listen to what People of Color want to tell us.

This chapter is short because this is not my story, it is the story of my brothers and sisters, members of my neurotribe, who live with prejudice and racism and erasure every day. As White Autistic Landon Bryce of *thAutcast* said about Black Autistic people (and, by extension, all Autistic People of Color),[13] "they are ours." They are our family. We are their family. We must listen to their story, we must make sure there is room at the table, we must value their voices. We must not talk over them. And above all, while not co-opting their stories or talking over them, we must stop thinking in terms of "them" because it's all just us. Just as we would wish for mainstream society to accept and welcome all Autistics as part of society while still honoring our differences, we must honor the differences of Autistic People of Color while recognizing that we are all members of the same family: the Autistic family. The human family. They are ours; we are us.

And that is why the essay for the letter C is so short. It is not that there isn't more to say– there definitely is. But I do not want to talk over or speak for my Autistic family members who are People of Color. I only want to remind everyone that they are here, they are among us, they *are* us. If our goal is, as I feel it should be, autism acceptance, we must remember that none of us are accepted until all of us are accepted. I challenge you to notice

13. URL: http://thautcast.com/drupal5/content/what-if-media-treated-black-people-way-they-treat-autistic-people

the color of autism as you look around our community and I challenge you to do whatever is in your power to add strength to the voices of People of Color– Autistic People of Color and their families. Until they are heard and until their needs are valued and until they are cherished as important members of our neurotribe we can talk about acceptance all day and all night but we will never find it.

I would like to leave you with a list of just a few of the Autistic People of Color and pro-neurodiversity family members and allies of Autistic People of Color who I know and respect to get you started on your journey of reading the voices of lived experience:

- Lydia Brown (blogs at *Autistic Hoya*, also served as the Autism Women's Network lead editor for the *Autism and Race* anthology)

- Mike Buckholtz (founder of Aid for Autistic Children Foundation)

- Kerima Çevik (blogs at The Autism Wars)

- Finn Gardiner (Institute for Community Inclusion, Boston. Autistic Self Advocacy Network)

- N.I. Nicholson (Editor-in-chief of *Barking Sycamores*, Coordinating Editor for NeuroQueer Books at Autonomous Press)

- Morénike Giwa Onaiwu (blogs at *Who Needs Normalcy*, Autism Women's Network project coordinator for the *Autism and Race* anthology)

- Kassiane Sibley (blogs at *Radical Neurodivergence Speaking*)

D is for Depression (and Anxiety)

No one can agree on how prevalent depression and anxiety are among Autistic children and adults, but, so far, everyone from professionals to parents to Autistics ourselves agrees that Autistic people are much harder hit by depression and anxiety than the general population. Some studies show more than a third of Autistic children are depressed[14] while the British report from the National Autistic Society (NAS), "You Need to Know" cites a study that found that 71% of Autistic children had one mental health issue and 40% had two or more.[15] One alarming study found Autistic children had 28 times as much suicidal ideation when compared to non-Autistic children.[16]

The studies of our depression and anxiety are still in their infancy at the moment. Researchers complain that it is harder to even determine if we are depressed at all because our facial expressions and methods of emoting are so different from the non-autistic population that a separate set of diagnostic criteria needs to be developed. Many of us "look depressed" all the time to those who are not familiar with our expressions. Many of us can move from feeling fine to clinical depression without it showing on our faces. Instead, observers might notice weight gain or loss, changes in patterns of activity, etc. Additionally, Autistics who have not yet developed reliable means of communication are not able to describe their mood to others. Communicative Autistics with alexithymia may not even be aware of our moods sufficiently to be able to clearly say if we are depressed or not.

One thing I am not seeing addressed enough is the question of whether our increased tendency toward depression and anxiety is a biological trait– another neurodivergence– connected to the genetics of autism or whether most of our mental health challenges are situational. Naturally, the reality will be a combination of the two, but I'm curious to know which of these two scenarios dominates. Of course, scientists aren't allowed to speculate in

---

14. URL: http://www.ncbi.nlm.nih.gov/pmc/articles/PMC3154372/

15. URL: http://www.autism.org.uk/get-involved/campaign/successes/reports/you-need-to-know.aspx

16. URL: http://www.sciencedirect.com/science/article/pii/S1750946712000931

public until they have conducted the sorts of studies that would tend to back up or refute their speculations, but looking through the scientific literature, I feel as if few people are ready to even begin examining any "inherent vs. situational" questions yet.

This is troubling, because I feel it is very important to know whether an Autistic neurology and biology are behind the higher rate of mood disorders or whether (as I strongly suspect) the bulk of depression and anxiety among Autistic children and adults could be alleviated through social understanding, adequate supports and accommodations, and autism acceptance. I do think the causes are ultimately a mix of biological and situational but I see clear evidence that, when it comes to autism and depression, situational causes dominate.

If you stop to think about all the reasons an Autistic person could be depressed, it's obvious that we live in a depressing world! The fact that we aren't all depressed all the time is a testament to the resilience of the human spirit and the persistence of Autistic people. If autistic depression is primarily an inherent neurodivergence that is more common among us, we can emphasize supporting and accommodating people experiencing depression, helping them to live happier and more satisfying lives. If autistic depression is primarily situational, we can emphasize improving our overall quality of life in order to lessen the depressive triggers. Optimally, society will choose to do both. But there is little point in supporting a depressed person while doing nothing to relieve the injustice in their life. Neither should we blame people who remain depressed even after their barriers have been removed. But I would argue that we absolutely must work to remove disabling barriers in Autistic people's lives if we ever hope to be able to relieve the high levels of depression and anxiety that Autistic people live with every day.

What sort of barriers am I talking about? To start with, we live in an uncertain world. That is something that increases everyone's anxiety, but Autistic people tend to have a more pronounced need for order, predictability, and a sense of control in our lives that goes beyond the level of these needs in most non-autistic people. Since anxiety is closely linked with depression, lowering anxiety levels should lower depression levels. For example, I have a friend whose young Autistic daughter becomes very anxious when someone uses the stove. I'm not sure what the source of her anxiety is. It seems to be linked to stirring things in pots, so maybe there is a sensitivity to the sound of the spoon scraping the pot? Or maybe something else happened one day while her mother was stirring something on the stove and the two events became linked in her mind. On a certain level, though, it doesn't matter why the daughter becomes distressed by cooking. All that matters is that her anxiety goes through the roof when she sees someone cooking.

Her mother's solution? Simple: Stop using the stove. Okay, maybe that's not so simple, but Mom has found other ways to cook food and keep the family fed and she says it is worth the extra effort because her daughter is so much less anxious and depressed now that she has a greater sense of certainty about the kitchen. People make comments like, "you'll get tired of accommodating her!" but her mother sees so much benefit in eliminating a huge source of stress from her daughter's life she is glad to be able to do something so small, in the grand scheme of things, in order to help her daughter grow up feeling more secure and happy. Maybe someday the "stove phobia" will pass. Maybe not. What matters is that a little girl feels calmer and happier and has more room in her life for learning and loving.

Another depressing reality Autistic people live with is social isolation. The internet has helped bring many Autistic people together, and that sense of community and shared culture helps a lot, but the Autistic community cannot be everywhere that Autistics are. When I go out in public alone, I am one Autistic surrounded by a sea of mostly non-autistic people, most of whom have very little understanding of autism.

Our experience of social isolation begins very early in life. Speaking for myself, my levels of stress, anxiety, and depression were relatively minimal until I started school. There were stressful issues at home– my brother was diagnosed with cancer when I was four years old and died about a month before my seventh birthday– but when I started pre-school at age 4, I was not really aware of the intense events on the horizon in my home life.

I remember being very excited about school. I remember waking up on the day of my 4th birthday, running into the dining room, and jumping happily up into my mother's arms. "Do you know what today is?" she asked me.

"My birthday!"

"And what does that mean?"

"I get to go to school now!"

She laughed (I guess she was looking for a different answer?) and said, "not yet, but soon. You're old enough now, but we have to wait until the school year starts."

Unfortunately, school did not quite live up to my dreams. I was excited about school because I loved reading and because my brother already went to school and I wanted to do every single thing he did. I had picked my reading skills up from watching television shows like Sesame Street and Electric Company and from following along on the page when my parents read stories to us. When I got to school, I found there was no reading and the other children were loud, chaotic, and generally unpleasant. I would have to wait two years for reading instruction and by then my reading level was so advanced I found *Fun With Dick and Jane* to be a tedious bore. I spent a lot of time hiding under the table.

While I was self-isolating, it didn't make the social isolation any less painful. I wanted friends. I still want friends! And I still self-isolate when I am overwhelmed. Too often, I hear people say that Autistics don't want friends. Given the infinite diversity of human expression, I'm sure there are some Autistics who don't want friends. But I believe most of us do want friends and people too often misinterpret our reaction to being overwhelmed as a sign that we don't want friends at all.

Autism acceptance has a role here. When we understand and are aware of this sensory overwhelm that causes Autistic people to pull away from others, it might seem like the answer is to do something to "fix" the Autistic so they can tolerate lots of noise and movement and chaos and thus have friends. A whole lifetime could go wasted while trying to change the core neurological wiring that goes into sensory defensiveness. But with autism acceptance– the stance that we are different, we are disabled, but we are not broken or wrong and should be accepted and loved for who we are rather than for dreams of who we might be changed into– a more immediate solution is to arrange social situations where Autistic people can spend time with others one-on-one or in very small groups in quieter, calmer environments. I am middle-aged but still that same overwhelmed child is inside me. I would far rather spend time with one or two people in a quiet room or a beautiful natural setting than go to a party or try to socialize in a noisy coffee house.

In addition to overwhelm, there is stigma to deal with. Some people find the mannerisms of Autistic people off-putting, whether they know the person is autistic or not.   Some of the ways we pursue friendships are annoying or frightening to others who don't understand and think we are harassing or stalking them. Social customs dictate that people avoid or abuse us in those situations instead of speaking openly and honestly to us about how our behavior makes them feel. Autism acceptance increases the chances that people choose to communicate to us about the things we are doing that cause them to feel uncomfortable instead of just abandoning us or taking unpleasant action against us while we are left to wonder what it was that we did wrong. Low self-esteem, anger, shame, depression– these are very normal reactions to social scenarios in which we are genuinely trying to develop friendships and repeatedly get "slapped away" with little or no explanation.

Bullying, as discussed a couple of chapters back, is a huge problem for Autistic people of all ages and is another source of social isolation. If the bullies are powerful, not only do they make life a torment for an Autistic person, but they can make it less likely that others will reach out in friendship to an Autistic person, for fear of also becoming a target of the bully. I think most kids who stand by and watch bullying without doing anything about it are against bullying but are just relieved that they are not the bully's chosen victim. Others might also feel annoyed or threatened by the Autistic person's words and behavior that they don't understand and choose to stand by passively because they feel the Autistic person deserves the torment, even if they, themselves, are unwilling to administer the social punishments. Being bullied is very socially isolating. I have never felt so alone and unloved as I have during those times when I was being bullied and onlookers were either joining in or standing passively, doing nothing to help or support me.

A study conducted in England[17] found that only 1/3 of Autistic people reported feeling adequately supported by others. It is very depressing to have life difficulties and feel like no one, or too few people, are rooting for you to succeed. It is small wonder that depression rates are high among Autistics when a majority report that they feel they have no one on their side to help them through a difficult, challenging, and often frightening world. Another British study[18] found that 50% of parents believe their child is not in a school environment that suits their needs. And yet another found as many as 1/5 of Autistic children have been formally excluded from school at some point and 2/5 have been informally excluded.[19] That study resonated with me because I was expelled from school due to being an "unmanageable behavior problem" that the administration would prefer someone else be burdened with.

Too many Autistics grow up believing that they are the root of all their own problems. Too many are explicitly told that they are bringing their problems on themselves. I was told that I was to blame for the bullying I experienced. It's a harsh message, whether it's delivered explicitly or implicitly. Autistic people often hear the grim messages from groups like Autism Speaks and take those bleak messages to heart. It's a depressing burden to grow up hearing what a depressing burden one is. Awareness is important, but it is not enough. All awareness by itself accomplishes is that it gives people an excuse. Without acceptance and accommodation, becoming aware of someone's autism just leaves bullies saying, "See? I knew there was something defective about you."

And not just childhood bullies. I left a community a year or two ago because I saw someone being bullied and I stood up for them. The bully said,

---

17. Page 22 of the study found at this URL: http://www.scie-socialcareonline.org.uk/the-way-we-are-autism-in-2012/r/a11G00000017tTEIAY

18. Cited in footnote 13 of the study in the previous footnote.

19. URL: https://www.ambitiousaboutautism.org.uk/understanding-autism/about-autism/stats-and-facts

"You don't understand. You're Autistic and having a meltdown. You don't get social things, so you can't possibly know what's really going on here." That is awareness without acceptance. That is autism being used as a bludgeon against the Autistic. That bully's "autistic awareness" was even harder on me than if they had known nothing at all of autism. Being aware of my autism only gave them a convenient way to shut me up when I tried to stand up for someone else they were hurting.

Yet we do need increased awareness of autism. What that means is that we really need increased acceptance of autism. The two go hand-in-hand: without awareness, there can be no acceptance. But without acceptance, awareness does immeasurable harm to Autistic people.

A final depressing point to touch upon is unemployment. Many, if not most, people derive a sense of self-esteem through feeling productive and useful. A British study found that 61% of unemployed Autistics said they want to work but only 15% of Autistics actually held full-time paid employment.[20] Once again, a big factor is stigma against autism and lack of acceptance and accommodation of Autistic workers. Of course unemployed Autistics are prone to depression. They are more likely to feel dissatisfied with life, more likely to experience social isolation, and more likely to live in poverty. When so many Autistics want to work but are unable to gain access to the support and accommodations needed for full-time paid employment, is it any wonder the rates of depression and anxiety are high among us?

There is not an epidemic of autism, but there is definitely an epidemic of depression and anxiety among Autistic people. There is strong evidence that much of this depression is situational and there is even stronger evidence that increasing autism acceptance will help to remedy much of what makes life so difficult for Autistic people. Yes, each Autistic person has their own pattern of strengths and weaknesses, but far greater than personal weaknesses are the stumbling blocks we find outside ourselves every time we interact with members of society at large.

The more that we are able to help people to see the great value of Autistic people– and not merely value tied to academic performance or

20. URL: http://www.autism.org.uk/professionals/employers.aspx

career skills, but inherent value, human dignity, and worth– the further along the road we will have traveled toward healing the depression and anxiety that so many Autistic people live with and suffer through every day.

E is for Empathy

I know, right?

The "empathy question" is one of the biggest enemies to autism acceptance. I read an award-winning philosophical treatise on the nature of autism, *The Ethics of Autism: Among Them but Not of Them* by Deborah R. Barnbaum, that claimed that Autistic people do not have empathy and therefore are not fully human. The author said that Autistic people could never develop community, due to this alleged lack of empathy. Moreover, the author made a philosophical argument that Autistic people should not be permitted to vote because our supposed lack of empathy meant we could not truly be citizens in the fullest sense of the word and had no place participating in the decisions of the nation. This isn't some fringe book– like I said, this book won several academic awards. And Temple Grandin wrote the foreword to it! I can only hope she was really busy that week and didn't have the chance to actually read the text, because she has said so many other things that do not agree with the message of that book.

News reporters tell audiences the "truth" about our lack of empathy. Every time there is a mass killing, experts are trotted out to speculate about the possibility of the killer being on the autism spectrum (and, in most cases, the killer turns out not to be Autistic) . . . because "everyone knows" about our stunning lack of empathy and who is more likely to kill lots of people than someone with no empathy? Right?

This is so very damaging. People who have never met me have said I cannot enter their house simply because they know I am Autistic and they saw a frightening news story about a killer. It is long past time to put the "empathy question" to rest. Here's the short version of the "empathy answer" for you: of course we have empathy!! It doesn't look the same as your (non-autistic) empathy, but we have it. And even if we didn't have empathy, it would not be a justification to dehumanize us and make our lives more difficult, or even to kill us, as some parents have done, sometimes ironically citing an alleged lack of empathy in the victim as motivation for the murderer's actions.

Okay, maybe the short answer wasn't so short after all.

Now for the longer version.

The first thing to think about when considering the empathy of Autistic people is the definition of empathy. The simplest definition of empathy is "the ability to understand and share the feelings of another." It looks simple, but right away we can break that into two parts: understanding other people's feelings and sharing other people's feelings. Autistic people can do both of those things but, like many other aspects of everyday life, we sometimes need a little assistance, mentorship, and accommodation. We also need a lot of awareness and acceptance on the part of others. Our empathy is obvious if you understand what you are seeing, but so few people really do understand us.

I'm not the first person to break empathy down into two separate processes. Academic/medical fields, including neuroscience, speak of "cognitive empathy" and "affective empathy." Cognitive empathy loosely correlates to the "understanding" half of the definition above, while affective empathy corresponds to the "sharing" half. These are two very different cognitive and emotional abilities, so, even though they are interrelated and both have a contribution to the aspects of autism that cause others to misunderstand our capacity for empathy, I need to consider them one at a time.

Cognitive empathy means knowing how someone else is feeling. We cannot share their feelings if we cannot see or understand them. There are many reasons why we can have difficulty seeing how someone else is feeling.

Some people will bring up an idea that says we cannot see other people's emotions because we do not have theory of mind. To have theory of mind is to understand that other people have minds and that those minds contain thoughts, knowledge, ideas, and desires that are different from the thoughts, knowledge, ideas, and desires in our own minds. It is this belief that we have no theory of mind that led John Horgan, former science writer for *Scientific American*, to declare in 1999 that "autistics often seem to make no fundamental distinction between humans and inanimate objects, such as tables and chairs."[21]   Never mind what seems true to Horgan, it is obvious that he doesn't know us. If I ever meet Horgan, I'll be tempted to ignore whatever he says and ask someone else if the sofa just spoke.

The idea that we lack theory of mind is a false one that goes back to something called the "Sally-Anne Test." Children were shown a situation in which two dolls, named Sally and Anne, had a marble. Sally puts the marble in a basket and leaves the room. While she is gone, Anne moves the marble from the basket to a box. The children were asked where Sally would look for the marble when she returns to the room. Of course, the answer the researchers are looking for is that Sally will look in the basket. If a child says that Sally will look in the box, the children are assuming that Sally has access to the content of the children's minds and can see things that happened while Sally was out of the room. The assumption in this case is that the child is lacking in theory of mind– the understanding that other people have different thoughts and perspectives from their own.

Typically developing children "fail" the Sally-Anne test until around age four or five. Children with Down Syndrome show a similar pattern, easily grasping Sally's different perspective on things by around age four or five. But in one study, conducted by Doctors Simon Baron-Cohen, Alan M. Leslie, and Uta Frith in 1985, around 80% of Autistic children were not able to pass the Sally-Anne test, despite having a higher testable IQ than the typically-developing and Down Syndrome age peers used as controls.[22]

This single study has been cited again and again and extrapolated to all Autistic people, not just young children. The thing that is forgotten is that autism is a developmental disability but not an absence of development altogether. Just because 80% of the children tested by Baron-Cohen, Leslie,

21. *The Undiscovered Mind: How the Human Brain Defies Replication, Medication, and Explanation* by John Horgan, Simon & Schuster, 1999, page 228
22. URL: http://ruccs.rutgers.edu/images/personal-alan-leslie/publications/Baron-Cohen%20Leslie%20&%20Frith%201985.pdf

and Frith could not pass the Sally-Anne Test at that point in their development, it does not follow that they never will or that no other Autistic people will develop theory of mind at some point in their lives. Fewer Autistic teens fail the Sally-Anne Test. Almost all Autistic adults who have means of communication (which is to say, the majority of Autistic adults) are able to easily pass the Sally-Anne test.

Theory of mind is not a simple on-off switch but rather a wide range of skills that are developed over time. Children who are born Deaf and not provided with sign language in early life not only struggle with language acquisition later but also fail the Sally-Anne Test at a later age than hearing children. Yet I have had many friends who were born Deaf and not provided sign language until later in life who demonstrated plenty of theory of mind by the time I met them as teens or adults.

More recently, researchers have discovered that Autistic children are not failing the Sally-Anne Test so much as the Sally-Anne Test is failing Autistic children. In 2013, researchers in Queensland, Australia, devised a new test for theory of mind called the "Dot-Midge Test."[23] It is based on the Sally-Anne Test, but with a significant difference: the test is made into a game in which the child stands the chance of winning a toy. Just as in the Sally-Anne Test, Midge hides the toy, then leaves the room. Dot then moves the toy. The difference is that the child is told that they are in a contest with Dot and Midge. First, the child chooses either Dot or Midge to look for the toy. If they find it, they get to keep it. If they don't find it, the child gets a turn to look for the toy. Again, if the child finds the toy, the child can keep it, but if the child does not find the toy, they don't get to have it.

When Autistic children were given the Sally-Anne Test, with the only motivation being getting the right answer, only 13% passed. But when the children were given the Dot-Midge Test with the motivation being to win a prize, 74% passed– choosing Midge to go first because the child knew that Midge had a false idea of where the toy would be. Neither of these percentages are in line with random chance– they are both far enough away from 50% to make it clear that something is inadequate about the Sally-

---

23. URL: http://www.ncbi.nlm.nih.gov/pubmed/23587041

Anne Test. (Some researchers speculate that the standard "reward" in the Sally-Anne Test, i.e. the social reward of being pleasing to the researchers, is not enough reward for the average Autistic child to be willing to work the problem through sufficiently.) It also becomes clear that there is a whole lot more theory of mind going on in the Autistic brain than has previously been credited.

So if we Autistics have theory of mind after all, why do we struggle so much with seeing people's emotions? This is an important question. I am saying that we do have empathy but we often don't realize that there is something to be empathetic about, so it is important to talk about why we miss those social cues.

One barrier is the ability to read and interpret facial expressions and body language. I think I have gotten pretty good with that skill, but I have worked at it for 40+ years and I still can't really do it in real time. I can interpret facial and body language in a video (though not in still photographs), most easily in fictional video– television and movies. Because I have high motivation and strong visual memory skills, I can re-play a real-life experience after the fact and generally, given enough time, figure out what happened. But I am clueless in the moment and sometimes the amount of time it takes me to decipher an experience is measured in months, not minutes. This is because I am not really using the same brain circuits that non-autistic people use when they interpret facial and body language. For non-autistic people (who do not have some other neurological divergence that affects reading body language) figuring out what someone is feeling by looking at them and listening to the tone of their voice is nearly instantaneous. There is no real effort involved. It just "happens" I have found that most people can't even explain how they know what they know when it comes to interpreting the vocal tone, facial expression, and body language of others.

When I try to interpret what is going on inside someone, it takes a lot of effort. I have to analyze the details of their posture and voice and apply logic and memory of many years of studying many books about body language. It takes so much effort that I just cannot do it in the middle of an interaction with someone. Sometimes I have only realized what was happening on the emotional landscape years after a conversation took place. Many past interactions are still mysteries to me. I have an easier time picking out emotions in movies and television shows because actors are intentionally broadcasting their body language loudly– the physical version of "speaking from the diaphragm," so to speak. I have put, and still do put, a tremendous amount of effort into learning to read body language and I am still really, really bad at it. And I accept that I always will be. I still work to learn what I can, but I know I will never approach "normal" levels of interpretation. Ever. In my entire life. And I'm (mostly) okay with that.

Brian R. King talks about the futility of trying to teach body language interpretation to Autistic children in his excellent book, *Strategies for Building Successful Relationships with People on the Autism Spectrum: Let's Relate!*:

> "My greatest frustration with the social skills classes of my experience is their insistence on trying to get our kids to make their brains do things that their brains do not do– recognize nonverbal communication, recognize vocal tone, recognize body posture and body language. If your brain does not pick that stuff up, you cannot make it. People have told me my entire life to look at body language, expression, and look at this, look at that. Guess what? It doesn't work and I will explain to you the reasons why that is and what you can do about it."

King goes on to do just that– explain the difficulties and give solutions. The best solution for not being able to read body language? Teach the non-autistic people to make their feelings explicitly known and teach the Autistic people to check-in with others to explicitly ask what they are feeling. You will find that Autistic people have a tremendous amount of empathy when we understand the emotions around us! You cannot claim we have no empathy when there are no accommodations in place to help us understand the emotional content surrounding us.

Another issue is alexithymia. Alexithymia is the word for not being able to recognize and put words to internal emotional states. People with alexithymia do have emotions, but we have a difficult time telling the difference between physical conditions, like illness, and emotional conditions with physical manifestations, like sorrow. Anyone can have alexithymia for a variety of reasons (PTSD from emotional trauma is a common cause.) Approximately 10% of the general population has alexithymia, but studies indicate that as many as 85% of Autistic people have some degree of alexithymia and an estimated 50% of us have severe alexithymia.

This is why I so often stress helping Autistic children learn what their emotional states are. All children can benefit from emotional mentoring, but Autistic children are in extra need of this sort of assistance. "It looks like you didn't like it when your sister took your toy away. I see your face is red and you are crying. Are you feeling angry? Are you feeling sad?" Conversations like these can help children learn to put names on their emotional states and can help them to recognize the physical symptoms of emotions. This latter is very important– I am nearly 50 years old and I still don't know when I am agitated or upset unless I remember to watch for symptoms like rocking back and forth more than usual, tense muscles, a churning sensation in my chest, tears, and so on. I have emotions, but I am not able to see them very clearly, so I have to apply logic to understanding my own emotions just as I apply logic to understanding the emotions of others.

Our primary difficulties with empathy lie in the realm of cognitive empathy. Help us understand what you are feeling. Help us understand what we are feeling. Help us to see a bigger emotional picture and you will find that we are very empathetic. Some researchers have suggested that, when it comes to affective empathy, not only are we not deficient, but we have more than usual– sometimes too much.

Affective empathy– the ability to feel "with" someone– is strong in most of us.   Henry and Kamila Markram have put forth a concept called the Intense World Theory.[24]   The idea is that the autistic brain is "supercharged"

24. URL: http://www.ncbi.nlm.nih.gov/pmc/articles/PMC3010743/

with many more neural connections than the non-autistic brain and, as a result, the world is too intense to bear. Sounds are too loud and painful, lights are too bright, smells are too strong, and feelings are too intense. The more intense the perception of the world, the more the Autistic person pulls away and builds a sort of "bubble" around themselves for protection. While most non-autistic people are able to "filter" the world so that it isn't so overwhelmingly intense, Autistic people get a massive flow of all data simultaneously and need to "shut off" in order to cope with it all.

Emotions coming from within can be just as overwhelming as sensory input coming from outside. If we cringe from the strong feelings of others and shut down at the strong feelings in ourselves when confronted with the strong feelings of others, we are not demonstrating a lack of empathy. We are demonstrating extreme sensitivity that should be recognized and respected. When we express empathy or sympathy by taking things to a cerebral level and doing research to try to help you with your struggles, we are not being "cold and clinical," we are showing our love in a way that is healthy and safe for us. Do not expect us to harm ourselves in order for you to feel as if we care about you. Respect our ways of being, our ways of knowing, our ways of loving.

But what I said above? Maybe we don't have empathy? Well.... maybe we don't. Maybe what I think is empathy in myself is actually sympathy. I have no objective way of knowing. All I can say is that I do care and I have seen countless other Autistics of all ages and walks of life expressing that they care. Isn't it enough to care, no matter what that caring actually is (sympathy, empathy, logical conclusions) or how that caring is expressed?

Don't stop with this chapter. Many other Autistics have written about the empathy question and at least one author I deeply respect, Cynthia Kim, has suggested that she really doesn't have empathy. In her essay, "The Empathy Conundrum," (*Musings of an Aspie*, January 17, 2013) Kim writes, "the subtle implication in the discussion about empathy that there is a right way to be autistic and that right way includes having empathy or too much empathy. And perhaps as a corollary to that: autistics who have too much empathy are doing their part to subvert the stereotype of the unfeeling autistic." What Kim says is so important. It goes against so much of what I said above and it is important for a couple of reasons. One big reason you need to go read the entire essay is because you cannot understand the "Autistic voice" unless you are open to listening to Autistic people. I have tremendous respect for Cynthia Kim and reading her very honest essay about empathy only raised my level of respect for her. How bold and vulnerable her writing is!

Another reason Kim's essay is so important is that it takes a different position concerning autism and empathy. Instead of defending our worth and attempting to allay public fears by insisting that we have empathy, Kim suggests that these attempts to make us appear "normal" end up oppressing many Autistic people by serving as a "hoop to be jumped through" in order to prove that Autistic people are "not that bad." I see her point. Once again, our worth is judged by how well we can conform with pre-existing definitions of what good, valuable, acceptable, allowable human expression has been determined to be, based on a mainstream model that profoundly privileges neurotypical expressions and values based on those expressions.

Go read Cynthia Kim's full essay. And in that essay, she links to another essay about empathy that you should read as well. Don't stop with mine. Or Cynthia's. Or the one she linked to. Read more. Learn more. Formulate your own ideas about autism and empathy. If you take away only one idea from me to inform you in that adventure of exploration, let it be that we are human beings with real emotions, real needs for support, and deserving of real respect and dignity. Do not let all that speculation about whether we have or lack empathy cause you to lose your own empathy in considering us. Thank you.

F is for Facilitated Communication

I'm cheating a little bit with my choice of the letter F for this topic. I want to talk about more than just traditional facilitated communication, but

I wanted to reserve C (communication) for Color and A (alternate communication) for Acceptance. Plus, I have seen facilitated communication getting a really bad rap in a lot of places, so I especially wanted to put it front and center, to take the opportunity to focus on why facilitated communication is important and necessary and why I'd like people to approach it with a more open mind. Stop giving it, and the people who use it and similar methods of supported typing, such a hard time.

Facilitated communication is often condemned as a fraud, with detractors claiming that the facilitator is using Autistic people (and other people with movement disorders) as puppets. For example, in 1994 the American Psychological Association (APA) released a resolution denying the efficacy of facilitated communication. Yet methods of supported typing are still very popular. Why? Because there are many people out there with movement and focus difficulties who are actually communicating their own words and thoughts, but who need assistance and accommodation to do so. Critics claim that people using facilitated communication could not communicate so well because they could not have taught themselves to read and write, but I taught myself to read beginning at age 2, so it is easy for me to believe that others are self-taught as well. I am not a different species– I am a human being and the things I have done are accessible to many other human beings as well.

Are some cases of facilitated communication or supported typing "puppet shows?" I think it's unlikely, but I haven't seen every single case so I just can't say it never happens. I have watched a lot of facilitated communication and I am friends with people who communicate through facilitated communication or related methods that include physical support and I am not one bit skeptical. I know I am talking to my friends, not to the people who help them with body pressure, helping them to stay upright and mobile, or helping them to stay focused on the task they want to accomplish.

Have you ever seen supported typing? If you have access to the internet, I would like you to go to YouTube to watch some videos of supported typing for yourself.

First, look for a video that's 11 minutes and 10 seconds in length, uploaded on October 5, 2011 and titled *Facilitated Communication - "I would not get to this stage if I did not get full support initially."*[25] This is sixteen-year-old Tim Chan from Australia, facilitated by his mother, Sarah. He began with wrist support (a method demonstrated about halfway through the video clip) and, over time, has progressed to only needing a supportive hand on his shoulder. The goal of many people who use supported typing is to eventually transition to being able to type without a facilitator at all. Today, Tim Chan types independently, without any physical support. I feel that the large number of people who began typing with support and eventually moved to independent typing without a change in the tone or content of their writing stand as strong evidence that facilitated communication can be real communication and not just using a person as a "puppet." Even if some cases of facilitated communication or other supported typing actually are frauds, the number of cases that are clearly not fraudulent imply that we should treat all supported typists with dignity and the presumption of competence.

Notice that part of the support Tim is getting is the help in staying on task. That can be very important for Autistic people and does not indicate that the facilitator is controlling him. Tim clearly wants to communicate– even when he goes to roll on the floor, he gets up again right away when another question is asked. I really understand his distractibility because I am the same way. I have a stronger level of focus which allows me to do things like safely drive a car, but my support needs are low enough and my motor skills are high enough that the knowledge of the seriousness and danger of what I am doing are sufficient to keep me focused when driving or using a sharp knife or any other similar potentially risky activity. But I know one person who began communicating using an accommodated form of typing who may be able to drive a car when she gets old enough because she can do trapeze work now– work that requires a lot more focus and coordination than I have.

When I am writing, or cooking, or drawing, or eating, I frequently get distracted and wander off. It is hard to stay on task. Obviously, I do stay

25. URL: https://www.youtube.com/watch?v=279h9QJ9ptw

enough on task to complete essays and art and to keep myself fed well enough to function (most of the time). I need less support in my everyday life than many other Autistics. Tim needs that support to help him stay focused and not walk off in the middle of a sentence. It is clear to me that Tim appreciates the support in focusing because I do not see signs that he is becoming agitated or being forced to do something against his will.

Next I'd like you to watch the trailer from the excellent film *Wretches and Jabberers*. You can find the clip by looking for the 2 minute and 32 second video uploaded on June 11, 2010 and titled *Official Wretches & Jabberers Trailer (Captioned)*.[26] In this clip you can see Larry Bissonnette and Tracey Thresher typing with support, and speaking– mainly by typing what they want to say and then reading their own words.

I would like everyone to see this film! It is so clear that the Autistic people in the movie who type to communicate are the ones who are making the words, not the facilitators who support them. Supported typing is not some kind of P. T. Barnum circus trick, and it is disrespectful and dehumanizing to say that Autistics who need a lot of support could not have thoughts to communicate, or suggest that those thoughts can only be believed if someone who needs a great deal of support in other aspects of their life does not need support around communication issues.

Facilitated Communication, which began as an assistive method of communication for people with cerebral palsy, was first developed in Australia in the 1970s by Rosemary Crossley. Building on that foundation, Soma Mukhopadhyay developed the Rapid Prompting Method (RPM) in the 1990s, first to help her son, Tito (who now types independently), and later to help many other Autistic people communicate. You can see a video explaining RPM and showing the use of a letter board for typing by looking on YouTube for a 4 minute video uploaded on October 28, 2014 and titled *RPM – how it's helping non-verbal autistic children*.[27]

And you can watch a video of my friends, Emma and Ariane by looking for a 9 minute and 44 second video published on YouTube on April 15,

---

26. URL: https://www.youtube.com/watch?v=2FllyJJRc0E
27. URL: https://www.youtube.com/watch?v=6c05Qq5WQew

2014 and titled *AZ and E 4 2 14*.[28] First Ariane reads something Emma
has written, and then we get to watch Emma's process of communication,
using Soma's RPM method. Emma can now type and write independently
and is the co-director of a documentary, *Unspoken*, which is coming out in
2016. I hope you will watch Emma's film. She is brilliant and creative and
well worth watching.

So, now that you've seen what these sorts of assisted typing look like, I
hope you are not as skeptical about their legitimacy. Why do other people
have a problem with assisted communication?

One reason is probably because they have seen something more
overbearing. I have heard of facilitated communication that is literally hand-
over-hand like some of the life skills training, such as brushing one's teeth. I
think if I had ever seen that method used for communication I might be
skeptical, too. I am not saying that the more hand-over-hand
communication styles are fraudulent. I am only saying that the types of
communication I have observed look much more like something that would
be nearly impossible to manipulate as if working with a human puppet.

Some people are skeptical because they find it too difficult to presume
competence when someone's body moves in ways they do not value. They can
accept Stephen Hawking's intelligence because he was not always so physically
incapacitated, but they struggle to accept the intelligence and competence of
someone whose body was always moving in scattered and unusual ways.

In a November 7, 2012 interview with Shannon Des Roches Rosa on the website
Thinking Person's Guide to Autism, my friend Amy Sequenzia explains why she
needs the support to type:[29]

"Typing, for me, is not a simple thing. I need to focus and try to make
my body and my brain work together. Sometimes I can't do that.
Sometimes I need a lot of physical support, sometimes I need very little.
I can type a few words independently, although this does not happen

28. URL: https://www.youtube.com/watch?v=RD805XUuF8c
29. URL: http://www.thinkingautismguide.com/2012/11/interview-amy-sequenzia-on-facilitated.html

very often, yet. I always need emotional support and encouragement."

If you'd like to read more of Sequenzia's thoughts and experiences, look for Ariane Zurcher's *Huffington Post* interview with Amy, "An Interview With Amy Sequenzia, a Non-Speaking Autistic Writer and Poet" (September 11, 2012).[30]

Some people don't see why a person would need support. As Kim Wombles wrote in "Facilitated Communication: Bandwagon Endorsements; It All Feels Good,"[31] her April 4th, 2011 critical review of *Wretches and Jabberers*, "Can someone explain why a man who has the fine motor skills to paint needs someone holding onto him to type?" She was speaking of the artist Larry Bissonette, who does now type independently. It seems obvious to me that things like making coffee, painting, and communicating through typing are three different skills and being competent or even highly skilled in one does not necessarily mean a person is going to be equally skilled in all three tasks. Obviously, Larry needed the support and encouragement of supported typing to help him as he developed greater communication skills.

I can draw, but my handwriting is nearly completely illegible. I am able to produce very readable handwriting if I "draw" it, but that takes so much longer than most people allot for handwriting that I am unable to succeed on hand-written exams and I had to switch to a different major because I could not finish mathematics exams in time– I would know the answers to all the problems, but would have to "draw" my work very slowly to avoid copying errors and be sure that the examiner could read my work. As a result, when time was called I had only worked through half the problems.

The same argument about support could be made for me. I can make coffee and I can draw– why do I require support and accommodations when it comes to handwriting? The simple answer: because I have a handwriting

30. URL: http://www.huffingtonpost.com/ariane-zurcher/autism_b_1871276.html
31. URL:http://www.science20.com/countering_tackling_woo_and_science_asds/facilitated_commu
nication_bandwagon_endorsements_it_all_feels_good-77796

disability: dysgraphia. My difficulties with fine motor control do show up in my drawings, but because I am able to take as long as I need to complete a drawing (I take lots of breaks because holding a pen is very painful for me) and because people seem to see a "primitive art" charm in my wobbly lines, the dysgraphia is not as impairing when I am drawing a giraffe as it is when I am required to write a grocery list, a letter, or an exam.

I like to give people some sort of litmus test for considering controversial things in the world of autism and here is my suggestion about supported typing, RPM, and facilitated communication: when you look at people who type independently now, did their "voice" change significantly from how they wrote when someone was holding their arm or shoulder? If your child is learning to communicate in a supported manner, do they seem happier and calmer? Does it look like they are getting more of their needs met? The most important gauge of truth when it comes to communication is "where the rubber meets the road." Is the supported typing or other controversial communication method making the person's life better? If the answer appears to be yes, stick with it and see where it goes. Ignore the naysayers and focus on what is helping you, your children, and your family.

There is plenty of evidence to use to gauge whether real communication is occurring. In the case of those folks who now write and type independently, it is clear that they have been the ones communicating all along. In the case of other folks who still need support, I feel it is best to presume that real communication is occurring there as well. Too many times, someone has been written off as "not being in there" only to later prove that they were, indeed, "in there" and were not so happy about being written off like that. The least harmful assumption is always that someone really is "in there" and that communication that seems to be coming from them is really their communication.

Even before someone develops independent typing (if ever, it is not a tragedy if they require support in communication for the rest of their life) there are strong indicators that real communication is taking place. Watch for those signs and, in the meantime, trust that you really are connecting with the person you seem to be connecting with. I am convinced that supported typing is valid. You may not yet be convinced as well, but if you love someone Autistic who is learning to communicate with support and assistance, you owe it to your loved one to trust their communication, support their process, and listen in love.

G is for Giraffe

If you ask most people what the symbol of autism is, they will say it is the puzzle piece, or they might talk about Light It Up Blue. Maybe they think the blue puzzle piece is the symbol or maybe the interlocking field of puzzle pieces in red, yellow, and two shades of blue.

The problem with all those symbols is that they were chosen by people who were not Autistic. A bigger problem with those symbols is that many Autistic people are offended by them, especially the puzzle piece. Some people would use a puzzle piece to symbolize Autistic people because they find us so puzzling. That is a short-sighted view. The puzzle piece is not rightfully a symbol of us Autistics because *all* humans are puzzle pieces. We are made for connection to one another. When people are not just aware but accepting of one another and of the multi-faceted beauty of our differences, we can find the ways we all fit together. We are all, every one of us, pieces of a picture so much larger than ourselves. If it were possible to pull back and see the glorious work of art our lives make when we connect in respectful acceptance with one another, the sight would be dizzying, infinite. So do not call us Autistics puzzles as if we were somehow separate from the greatest mysteries and joys of humanity. Know that we belong here. Know that we are not among you, we *are* you. All humans are different– the word "neurodiversity" encompasses every human brain there ever was and ever will be. Yes, we Autistics are neurodivergent– different in particular ways that diverge from the majority. But do not allow yourself to become so dazzled by our differences that you forget that we are part of your family, part of the human family. To resist autism acceptance is to resist accepting the total beauty of the human spirit in all its fiery glory.

But the puzzle piece symbol is theirs, not ours. G is for Giraffe because the giraffe is one of the symbols of autism that was chosen by Autistic people ourselves. In this chapter, I'm going to talk about some of our symbols– the giraffe, the infinity symbol (sometimes portrayed as a Möbius infinity symbol), the spectrum rainbow, and the color red. I will also take time to explain why the puzzle piece and the color blue are not our symbols.

The giraffe is a beautiful symbol because it comes from Autistics speaking up against a song with defamatory language. Therefore it is a symbol of Autistic power. The giraffe comes from Autistic people staying calm while being compared to lamps and animals and being told that they live in a prison of their neurology. The giraffe is Autistic people turning something so offensively ridiculous and ridiculously offensive into a big joke – using laughter to battle ignorance and non-acceptance like the heroes of the Harry Potter series of novels fought their fears with the Riddikulus charm. Therefore the giraffe is a symbol of Autistic joy. The giraffe was rapidly adopted by a large number of Autistics, almost overnight. Therefore, it is a symbol of Autistic community.

For a brief moment, the dandelion was our symbol, but therapists and corporations quickly stepped in and took that symbol and subverted it for their goals, including, in at least one case, adding in the divisive claim that the dandelion symbolized "high functioning" autistics. If a symbol is not for all of us, it is not our symbol. If a symbol implies or demands "functioning labels," it is not our symbol. Symbols of Autistic culture must always represent solidarity among us, because Autistic culture values acceptance and inclusion. If you ever see someone trying to take our giraffe away like our dandelion was, please step in, say something, stop them. The giraffe connects us all and must never be used as a symbol of dividing our community.

Another symbol that unites us is the infinity symbol, often shown as a ribbon or even as a Möbius ribbon (a ribbon with a single twist, becoming a model for a single-sided object in three-dimensional space because it has no front or back). And, yes, it too has been taken and subverted in unpleasant ways, but still belongs more to us than to those who have taken it and made it out of a puzzle-piece ribbon or made designs that put the infinity symbol and blue puzzle pieces together in piece of jewelry they sell, donating the profits to Autism Speaks.

The infinity symbol can be depicted in different colors, but it began with a rainbow spectrum of colors to symbolize the great diversity in the Autistic community. Many people use the rainbow infinity symbol to represent the full spectrum of human neurodiversity as well– neurodiversity being about the full range of neurotypes, not just autism.

The first place I remember seeing the spectrum infinity symbol was in the logo for AFF (*Aspies for Freedom* – a group that accepted and sought to unite all people on the spectrum, despite the potentially divisive name of the organization) in 2004. The symbol has been widely adopted and grown much larger than AFF in the years since the founding of that group.   AFF also established Autistic Pride Day (June 18th), which is still observed by many people in the Autistic community as a day that we can celebrate without the emotional difficulties so many of us experience in the month of April with the heavy emphasis on tragedy that comes with Autism Awareness Month.

Finally, the color red was chosen in 2015 as a bright and visible alternative to the Autism Speaks color, blue. The campaign is called Walk in Red and includes wearing red and blogging/tweeting/writing/celebrating Autism Acceptance. Not only is blue undesirable because it is the color of Autism Speaks, but blue is not inclusive, since Autism Speaks chose the color blue (from Rosco filters) to represent boys, automatically excluding women and girls:

> "The first question we wanted to ask was – why blue? What does the color blue have to do with the autism spectrum? The answer is that Autism Spectrum Disorders are almost 5 times more common among boys (1 in 54) than among girls (1 in 252). So, the color blue represents the boys diagnosed with autism." – Rosco's comments about being the

official shade of blue for Autism Speaks.[32]

As for that puzzle piece? From the beginning, it was meant to symbolize something missing from Autistic people. That is offensive. We are not missing or lacking parts. For Autistic History Month (November) 2013, Autisticook wrote about the history of the puzzle piece symbol in a blog entry titled "Autistic History Month: the puzzle piece" and published on her self-titled blog, Autisticook.[33] You can read more reactions to the puzzle piece symbol at Unpuzzled.net, too.

Symbols are vitally important. They carry meaning and help in the transmission of Autistic culture. Symbols can be oppressive judgments laid on us against our will or they can be vibrant and uplifting celebrations of our own choosing. If you have been using the puzzle piece to symbolize us, please read more about the history of the symbol and the reactions of many Autistic people. Yes, there are some Autistic people who choose the puzzle piece. That is their right. But ask yourself what you see the majority of Autistic people doing and ask yourself if it is your place to decide whether Autistics are justified in being offended or not.

If an Autistic person chooses the puzzle piece for themselves, do not tell them they are wrong, especially if you are not also Autistic. But if you are not Autistic and you are choosing to use the puzzle piece as a symbol of us, you need to ask yourself if that symbol is worth the number of people you are going to alienate with it. If you care about Autistic people, please think about getting rid of your puzzle pieces. No, they don't offend every Autistic. But do you really want to offend large numbers of us? If you want to be our ally, listen to us and do not speak over us. Do not tell us why you think we shouldn't be offended by the puzzle piece symbol. Don't try to justify using it because you think it's clever or pretty or appropriate in some way. Don't talk down to us as if we were incapable of understanding symbolism, and don't excuse your use of an offensive symbol with statements like, "but the order has already come back from the printer and we would have to re-

32. URL: https://www.autismspeaks.org/blog/2012/04/02/shine-light-autism-rosco-color-filters
33. URL: https://autisticook.wordpress.com/2013/11/30/autistic-history-month-the-puzzle-piece/

design everything to get rid of that symbol."

If it is important to you to be an ally to the Autistic community, truly be an ally to the Autistic community. Listen to us and don't assume that you know better than we do what we should call ourselves or how we should use symbols to represent ourselves. If you want to be our ally, support us.

H is for Healthcare Access

Healthcare access is a big topic today, thanks to the Affordable Care Act (ACA). I see people commenting often, either grateful for the ACA and their newfound healthcare access or angry about the ACA and their extra costs or lost access. What often gets lost in the shuffle are those groups that did not have good healthcare access before the ACA and have not been significantly helped by the passing of the ACA.

Autistic people have struggled to get our health needs met for a long time and will be struggling with our healthcare access for some time to come. In the wake of the passage of the ACA, the voices of adults responsible for securing their own healthcare are often drowned out by the voices of those who say the main need of Autistic healthcare consumers is 40 hours per week of ABA therapy. All the attention when it comes to our healthcare gets focused on children and ABA (Google "autistic health care" or "autism ACA" to see what I mean), and the genuine medical needs of both Autistic adults and Autistic children too often get swept under the rug. Too many of our basic health care needs are not getting met, and some aspects of autism make our difficulty accessing health care invisible in the public discussions.

As I see it, there are three main reasons why we are such an underserved population: bias against the value of Autistic lives, communication issues, and healthcare provider ignorance. And the three solutions are acceptance, accommodation, and awareness/education.

I think most people reading this don't need to be convinced that Autistic lives have value, but just in case, I'll say this: We are human beings. We have thoughts, feelings, desires. We want to be healthy and live long, full lives (our life-well-lived doesn't always look the same as a mainstream, non-autistic life-well-lived but that doesn't speak to our value as human beings.) We deserve the same respect, dignity, and chance in life as anyone else.

Doctors don't always feel that way, though. One example is the case of Mel Baggs, who had to fight in 2013 to get a GJ tube, an important feeding tube to counteract the effects of gastroparesis or paralyzed stomach. Mel would die without the tube, and the doctors knew that, and they were trying to encourage Mel to just go home and die. Mel's case because known on the internet and people from all over the country called the hospital to protest . . . and Mel got the tube and is alive today.

Mel wrote, "But I had to fight for this tube. Even though it was the only way to save my life. I had to fight against people who were certain I was better off dead. And I needed the help of a lot of people on the Internet, to do it. When I did get the tube, it was done without a working anesthetic. And even though the local anesthesia didn't work on me, even though I was yelling and screaming, they didn't stop to give me more, they just kept telling me that the Versed meant I wouldn't remember it later. Yeah right."[34]

(More on failed attempts to provide appropriate anesthesia to Autistics in a bit.)

Another example is 23-year-old Autistic Paul Corby, who was refused a heart transplant. Paul was in great health except for the left ventricular noncompaction in his heart. There is a long waiting list for hearts– several hundred people die every year while waiting for a heart. Paul was young, otherwise healthy, and a great candidate for a transplant . . . if only he didn't have autism. His life was valued so much less than the lives of others that he was not even allowed on the waiting list.

Three years later, Paul is still trying to get on a waiting list for a heart. In

34. Mel Baggs, May 2, 2013, "Feeding tubes and weird ideas." URL:
   https://ballastexistenz.wordpress.com/2013/05/02/feeding-tubes-and-weird-ideas/

the meantime, he has written three novels for young adults. Paul just wants to live, to be able to walk up a few steps without losing his breath and becoming exhausted, to continue to write and play video games and to watch his nephews grow up. As of October, 2015, his petition has over 297,000 signers but still he is not allowed on a transplant waiting list.[35]

These and so many other cases are prime examples of why we need increased autism acceptance. It is wrong for doctors to decide that it is better for someone to die because they have a developmental disability. Yes, there are risks with a feeding tube. Yes, there is a long waiting list for heart transplants. But Mel was willing to take those risks, and Paul deserves to be on that list. Transplant lists have triage codes to govern the speed with which people move up the list and it is wrong to not allow Paul on the list at all when he could have at least been sitting on a slow track for the last three years.

Communication issues are another serious barrier to getting healthcare needs met. In the case of non-speaking Autistics, communication issues often revert to barrier of perceived human value– those who do not speak are, quite unfairly, valued less by many people than those who do speak. But those of us who speak part- or full-time are often confronted with communication barriers as well.

Communication barriers include things like rushed appointments, in which we are not given sufficient time to process language or in which we are "punished" for "waiting so long to bring that up" when we had been struggling for the whole visit to get the important words out. Communication barriers include things like not being able to focus because of fluorescent lights or not being able to hear the doctor's words because of clanging medical equipment. We can't communicate symptoms well if our doctors ask the wrong questions, and we have sensory wiring that doesn't always allow us to know where our pain is or even that we do have pain. Sometimes doctors rush through instructions that are only given orally with no room for processing or remembering the information and no written record to help us recall what we were told. This is usually followed up with,

---

35. URL: https://www.change.org/p/help-my-autistic-son-get-a-life-saving-heart-transplant

"any questions?" and an overwhelmed and overstimulated Autistic often just says, "no," because there is not the time and mental space to process everything and access language quickly enough to form questions on the spot. Communication barriers can be invisible to doctors because we are so compliant that we say everything is good when it isn't or because we come across as so intelligent that it seems impossible to our healthcare providers that we could also have significant difficulties with communication. Communication barriers can even be invisible to ourselves if we are so overwhelmed that we aren't even able to know what we don't know.

Accommodations are the best answer to these sorts of barriers. One accommodation I use is a little digital voice recorder. I ask permission to record the consultation, saying, "my memory is like a sieve. This is just so I will remember what we talked about, okay?" I have not yet had a doctor refuse to allow me to record our visit. Later, I transcribe the recording into a text document because written language is so much easier for me to process than spoken language. I add the transcript to my personal medical file and I can quickly and easily see how long I was supposed to soak a body part for or what I was supposed to eat or not eat with those pills, etc. I also try to come into an appointment with printed out notes or a bullet list whenever possible. Some doctors seem put off by my bringing notes, but it is the only way I can be sure that my needs will be met in such an overwhelming environment.

For an excellent discussion of some of the accommodations that will help Autistic adults get better access to health care, read Cynthia Kim's essay, "Accessible Health Care for Autistic Adults," published June 3rd, 2014, on the *Autism Women's Network* website.[36] Many of her points spill over into my third topic: educating healthcare providers about the ways that Autistic people are unusual in a medical setting.

I already mentioned one of those: our unusual responses to pain. Our nervous systems often do not respond the way the nervous systems of non-autistic people respond. Sometimes a tiny splinter or a gentle bump causes unbearable pain. Sometimes a broken bone doesn't even register with us. We

36. URL: http://autismwomensnetwork.org/accessible-health-care-for-autistic-adults/

are both hypersensitive and hyposensitive to pain, and one person can be both hyper-and hypo-sensitive, depending on the setting, the injury, and what else we are currently coping with processing at the time. Health care professionals need to be very aware that not presenting with pain as a symptom does not necessarily rule out a diagnosis that normally requires pain to be present. And they need to be aware that when we express extreme pain from something that seems like it shouldn't hurt, we are not being "big babies," we are in genuine pain from a nervous system that is often quite unpredictable and gives us genuine and often intolerable pain in situations that someone else might judge "not painful."

On top of that, we are sometimes awake during anesthesia. We sometimes remember clearly what transpired during "twilight sleep." We sometimes under-respond to local anesthesia and are traumatized twice– once by the pain and a second time by health care professionals' response to our pain. I went without dental care for years because of a dentist who told me to stop screaming. "You don't want to scare the children, do you?" he said. "But *I'm* scared!!!" I said. He was pulling out one of my back molars– the ones that have the curved roots and have to be pulled out in several different directions, like a corkscrew. My mouth was not numb. It hurt tremendously, and I have a pretty high pain threshold– I gave birth to an eleven-pound baby with no medication and got up afterward and walked out of the room by myself. I was scared, I was in pain, and instead of comforting me or discussing further pain or anxiety management options, the dentist chose to shame and humiliate me for an honest and uncontrollable reaction to the situation.

I was not afraid of dentistry before that visit. After that visit, I could not even go to the dentist for a routine check-up or teeth cleaning. Health care providers fail to realize what severe trauma they can cause or what a huge negative impact they can have on a patient's overall health. And, once again, it is hard to find useful information about autism and dental anesthesia because parent concerns– such as the fear that anesthesia will cause or worsen autism– drown out the actual needs of actually Autistic people.

Education is the answer here. Health care professionals need to be aware of atypical responses to anesthesia and other medications. They need to be aware of issues like touch sensitivity and be educated about the importance of letting Autistic people of all ages know exactly what is going to happen beforehand. Many of us are easily startled. Many of us do not show extreme fear in ways that untrained people are able to recognize. Many of us can have overwhelming levels of panic or pain that medical professionals are unprepared to deal with. One way to help educate your individual health care providers (and, by extension, help them serve other Autistic people better as well) is to use the healthcare toolkit developed by AASPIRE (Academic Autistic Partnership in Research and Education).[37]

Lynn Soraya has a very important essay about the difficulty of dealing with health care professionals who do not understand autism, "Barriers to Effective Medical Care for Autistic Adults," published June 30, 2014, on *Psychology Today*.[38] It is required reading if you seek to even begin to understand what we go through when we try to get our healthcare needs met. Be sure to check out the pages she links to at the end of her essay (one of which is Cynthia Kim's essay, mentioned earlier in this chapter). So many of us have stories that range from very annoying to outright horror stories about being treated poorly by health care professionals who do not understand our needs or how our presentation can be so misleading to those with little or no experience with Autistic people.

Once again, autism awareness is not sufficient– it can make people feel good about "doing something to help," but it doesn't actually help. When it comes to our health care needs, Autistic people need better education for healthcare providers, better accommodations in the health care setting, and above all we need autism acceptance because we will never get our health needs met until we are fully recognized as deserving of respect and dignity, and until we are widely understood as being valuable not for what we can do, but for who we are: Your brothers and sisters, and fellow human beings. Until society is willing to own us as "one of us" instead of a frightening and dehumanized "them," we will continue to struggle and fight for the basic level of health care so many other people take for granted.

---

37. The toolkit is available at http://autismandhealth.org and I recommend it highly.
38. URL: https://www.psychologytoday.com/blog/aspergers-diary/201406/barriers-effective-medical-care-autistic-adults

I is for Identity-first Language

I know of several groups of people out there who want to be referred to by what's called person-first language. For example, "people with narcolepsy" is so common that it has a well-known abbreviation: PWN. I have watched discussions in diabetes forums in which people either don't care what they are called or insist very strongly that they should be called "people with diabetes" and never "diabetics."

People who feel strongly about person-first language tend to explain their stance by saying that they don't want to be identified with their disease. The disease is difficult and challenging and they don't feel like it is a part of who they are, but rather a tacked-on difficulty they cope with. It doesn't describe them, it doesn't define them, and they would be the same person with or without the condition– it is a surface-level layer that could be peeled away without removing anything significant about the person underneath.

Not only do I respect those groups' choice of person-first language, but I agree with them. I don't have narcolepsy but I have another serious sleep-related disability (hypernychthemeral syndrome, a.k.a. Non-24-Hour Sleep-Wake Syndrome) and while it doesn't bother me at all if someone refers to me as "an N24" rather than "a person with N24," it is not a deep-rooted part of who I am. If a miracle cure could remove my N24, I would be the same person I was before, just with a much healthier sleep pattern. It's not a part of who I am.

But autism is different. Autism is a pervasive developmental disability– it is pervasive, it pervades every part of my being. Autism is not a layer over top of a non-autistic person. Autism is a word to describe a different type of brain, with different wiring. Autism is a brain that is different in both structure and function. And as an amateur neurobiologist, I believe that my brain is who I am. Someone else might have religious views and say that their soul is who they are, but even they will likely admit that the material vehicle of that soul is seated in the brain. The brain is where thoughts come from. It is where the control panel is for the excretion of the biological chemicals that cause emotions to be experienced. When we see, hear, smell, feel, taste, it is our brain that tells us what we are sensing. Every part of the body comes back to the brain.

So, I cannot be separated from my autism. I've met people in the diabetes community who hate the phrase "my diabetes" and refuse to use it because they don't want to claim the disease as theirs, instead viewing it as an unwanted invader in their body. If I tried to say that about MY autism, I would be calling my own brain a foreign body that I want to eject. That sounds like the basis for a horror movie to me. It is MY brain! It has MY thoughts and MY feelings in it. It is filled with MY memories. I need MY brain. And MY brain is an autistic brain. It is MY autism. Mine.

So to call me a "person with autism" is, at best, disturbing to me. I strive to temper my reaction because I know that people have good intentions, but the good intentions do not make an offensive statement innocuous. It is still offensive to me when people say things like "fight autism" (you want to fight my brain? Why do you hate me?) or call me a "person with autism." (Why not call me a "person with a brain?" To me it is the same thing.)

One of the hallmarks of person-first language, as you may have noticed from the examples I used, is that it is a way to separate a person from something that is considered unworthy, unwanted, ugly, or undesirable. Narcolepsy is a difficult and challenging condition and the only positive I've noticed about it is the way it brings people together in a loving community that cares for one another. (I really do love the narcolepsy community! PWN are among my very best friends!) Diabetes is a similar case– there is nothing good about having a malfunctioning pancreas or metabolism and it makes sense to want to use language that separates that dysfunction from one's core identity.

But autism is not the same. It brings both challenges and rewards. My sensory challenges make the world a very painful place to live in, but they also bring an exquisite sensitivity that causes music to bring me to tears of ecstasy. I process spoken words more slowly than people around me but I process numbers and symbolic logic much more quickly. I have a hard time figuring out what emotions people are speaking with their face, tone of voice, body positioning but I develop strong and deep and loyal bonds to other people. I have difficulty regulating many of my body functions, such as heat and cold, and I can become overwhelmed by too much motion, light, sound, etc., but I have access to a deep, deep, deep joy by manipulating movement, light, sounds, etc. on my own.

Note that those are my personal pattern of weaknesses and strengths. Each Autistic person has their own balance sheet of challenges and joys– they don't all look just like mine. But this is the thing: We each have challenges and strengths. Autism isn't all negative. It isn't all challenge. And because autism is about the entire brain and how it is wired, it is not a thing that can be peeled away from us. If it were possible to rewire our brains and recode our genetics, the challenges might be removed, but the delights would go along with them. We would lose the parts of autism that lead us to struggle in a society that has difficulty understanding and accommodating us, but we would lose the joys of autism along with them. It's all tangled together into one big crazy quilt of identity– it is all a significant and rooted part of who we are. Without autism, we would not be who we are.

And this is why so many of us (although not everyone) ask that identity-first language be used to refer to us. That is why you meet so many Autistic adults and teens and children who ask to be called "Autistic," not "people with autism," because it really is a part of our identity. Every bit as much as (or more than!) our gender, our nationality, our hair and eye color, our career if we have one, our major at school if we attend. It is as deeply rooted a part of our identity as being a human being. It is simply who we are. If someone asks you to use person-first language when referring to their autism, of course you must respect that, but don't assume that an Autistic person wants you to use person-first language, and don't argue with those of us who choose identity-first language. I have grappled with people who insist I cannot refer to myself as Autistic. How rude it is to tell someone how they should identify themselves!

Respect the way people choose to self-identify. Many of us consciously choose to use identity-first language, identifying as Autistic. And some of us also choose to capitalize the A in Autistic as a statement of identity. Lydia

because I was crying in public. I usually have a handkerchief but I'd forgotten to carry one that day so I ended up blowing my nose on my gloves. I put the materials I had intended to buy back on the shelves and left. I had to sit in my car and calm down before I could safely drive the few blocks to a competitor's home improvement store, where I was treated with kindness and acceptance. I was feeling particularly emotionally fragile, but everyone in the second store was kind to me and one of the employees who helped me was visibly disabled, making me feel like I was in a store that respects and values disabled people as employees and as customers. Being treated better at the second store helped restore some of my dignity, but still I didn't sleep that night. I lay in bed, unable to chase away memories of being mocked for being different, unable to chase away tears of sorrow and shame.

Those men have probably long forgotten the "weird girl" they laughed at. I am still living with the emotional and physical consequences of the experience. I spent years trapped in schools full of bullies. There is a form of complex PTSD (C-PTSD) that emerges from a childhood of being daily trapped in an environment of physical and emotional torment. Today I am exhausted, nauseated, and haunted by memories I had thought I'd put behind me. For them it was a moment's amusement. For me it is days of recovery.

There were so many other J words on my list to choose from and "joke" was not originally one of them, but at the last minute, I knew that this was my word. I have been treated as a joke since childhood. No one should be treated as a joke! It is not okay to mock disabled people. Autism acceptance includes teaching people that we are not different on purpose and we do not deserve to be mocked for our differences. Making fun of us for the ways we don't fit in will not teach us to fit in (or shame us into fitting in). It will only make us feel sad or angry and excluded. In those without a strong sense of self, it will make us feel bad and wrong about who we are. The world has enough pain and suffering in it already. Choose to bring light and happiness into the world. Choose to make others feel better about who they are, not worse. Do not make cruel jokes about the people around you. Think very carefully before even indulging in the sort of casual ribbing based on mild insults I sometimes see others sharing in– we are sensitive and prone to misunderstanding your intentions. We have been mocked and bullied so long that some of us can no longer bear even friendly, good-natured teasing. Think carefully, treat us with dignity, help us to feel that we belong and are wanted. Choose acceptance.

K is for Kids (But Probably Not the Ones You Expected)

No, I don't mean all those Autistic kids. I mean Autistic people becoming parents and having kids of their own. Sometimes Autistics have Autistic kids, sometimes not. Either way, Autistics who become adults are nearly invisible and Autistics who become parents are even more invisible than that.

Autistic parents have a hard time finding each other. they have a hard time finding information about their own situation. Google "autistic parent" and most of what you will end up with are links to information about being a non-autistic person with Autistic kids. Lots of Autistic parents are keeping a low profile or are even "in the closet" if they are able to pass as non-autistic folks at all. There is a realistic fear of having one's kids taken away by a society and a government that believes Autistic people are not competent parents. Other Autistic parents struggle with people's attitudes– lots of people are very interested to hear about parenting Autistic children . . . until they realize that the information is coming from an Autistic adult. I would think people would be more, not less, interested in hearing what an Autistic person has to say about raising Autistic kids, but it turns out that, too often, that's not the case at all.

Since I am not parenting kids, I want to turn to the voices of those who are. My dear friend Lei Wiley-Mydyske has a lot to say about what it's like to be an Autistic adult parenting an Autistic kid. The way that people talk over and through Autistic people is doubled when they are talking to an Autistic parent of an Autistic kid. "They told me that I don't know how his brain works like they do, because they are behaviorists and professionals who know about special education and I am just a radical whose brain is flawed just like his." Lei writes in "They Don't Care About What We Say," on the *Parenting Autistic Children With Love And Acceptance* blog.[40] She is his parent. She is actually Autistic. And she is discounted, viewed as the person who knows the least about what he needs, because the school has autism awareness with no autism acceptance.

Being Autistic often means being shut out of our own lives. People want to listen to what everyone else has to say about autism, but they get dismissive or angry when actually Autistic people want to join the dialog that is about . . . . US! Can you imagine a world where only men are permitted to discuss women's issues? What if only whites were allowed to talk about black issues? But we do live in a world where (unless you're Temple Grandin) no one wants to hear what Autistics have to say about autism. We live in a world where the loudest voice about autism – Autism Speaks – actively works to silence the voices of actually Autistic people.[41]

What? You didn't know about that? The Autistic community got Google to change hate speech in their search engine and Autism Speaks reported it as something Google did, not something Autistic activists got Google to do.[42] Autism Speaks made a documentary about augmentative and alternative communication (AAC) and focused only on the parents and caretakers, shutting out and denigrating the voices of people who actually use AAC to such an extent that they did not even show Autistic people using AAC to communicate in a documentary about using AAC to communicate. Autism Speaks quoted an Autistic who protests them, twisting her words to make it appear as if she supports Autism Speaks, and persistently refused to remove her words for years.

But as upsetting as it is that Autism Speaks does this to us, it is even

---

40. URL: https://autloveaccept.wordpress.com/2015/03/23/they-dont-care-about-what-we-say/
41. For more information and research, including analysis from other Autistic writers, follow Boycott Autism Speaks on Facebook. URL: https://www.facebook.com/boycottautismspeaksnow/
42. Resource URL: http://yesthattoo.blogspot.com/2013/03/erased-silenced-derailed.html

more upsetting that the large organization is just echoing the way a majority of the general population respond to us. Look at the parenting blogs of non-autistic parents of Autistic kids and you will see that they have tens of thousands of followers. Look at the equally well-written blogs of Autistic parents of Autistic kids and you will see hundreds of followers. There are a few Autistic authors with a high readership, but the bloggers talking about parenting Autistic children from the perspective of being an Autistic parent? Whatever the digital equivalent is of crickets chirping, that's what's surrounding their words.

The Huffington Post ran a series of personal essays titled "Autism in our Family" and all the essays were written by non-autistic family members of Autistic people. Lei Wiley-Mydyske wrote and asked them why they had no Autistic voices and they invited her to submit an essay. She wrote about being an Autistic adult raising an Autistic child, and HuffPo turned it down. Now, while I think it's well-written, it could have been turned down for not being up to HuffPo's preferred level of writing quality, but I would have thought that the fact that it was an essay about raising an Autistic child while being Autistic one's self would make the essay valuable enough for HuffPo to be willing to work with the author to help make the essay meet their publishing criteria. But that's not what happened. And, once again, an actually Autistic voice went unheard.

You can hear her Autistic-parenting-an-Autistic voice now. Lei published her essay in its entirety on her blog. "Every day, my son and I face discrimination and stigmatization for being openly Autistic. For all the 'awareness' that is so popular now, there is very little understanding and even less in the way of authentic inclusion. We both need a lot of support in this world, and getting that support without being faced with a lot of hostility and resentment is difficult."[43]

Cynthia Kim is also a well-written Autistic parent. She interviewed many other Autistic mothers for a three-part article about parenting on the spectrum that you can find on the Autism Women's Network website.[44]

---

43. From "Autism and Activism in Our Family," on We Always Liked Picasso Anyway. URL: http://autistictimestwo.blogspot.com/2014/08/autism-and-activism-in-our-family.html

44. URL for part 1: http://autismwomensnetwork.org/motherhood-autistic-parenting/

"If you Google 'autism' and 'mother,' you'll find hundreds of references to mothers of autistic children for every mention of mothers who are autistic. It would be easy to assume– as perhaps many people have for a long time– that autistic mothers simply don't exist. But if you dig a little deeper, you'll find that not only do we exist, we have a unique experience of what it means to be a parent."[45]

"In reality, there are already many autistic parents. Yet we seem to be largely invisible when it comes to autism-related supports. Services are available for autistic children and for parents of autistic children and for autistic adults who live with their parents or in supported living arrangements. But supports for autistic parents, regardless of their children's neurology, are mostly absent from the landscape."[46]

"However, as an autistic parent, we have a secret weapon– one that can make our autistic children's lives less challenging than our own have been. Kim echoed the sentiments of many autistic moms, explaining how she and her autistic son have a special bond: 'We love and accept each other enough to be ourselves. I am able to help him put words to things he doesn't yet understand. I am able to help him figure out sensory issues that bother him and help him find solutions that work for him. I'm a problem solver and I work at something 'til all the kinks are worked out.'

"Acceptance and understanding were common themes when autistic mothers talked about their parenting strengths. 'It has been a huge benefit to have a shared neurology with my son,' says Puddy. Not only is she able to read his stress signals and coping levels, helping him to prevent escalations in his behavior, she says that 'he finds great comfort in the fact that I can understand his need for routines and stimming that others see as odd.'"[47]

K is for Kids and that's a realistic part of so many Autistic people's lives.

---

45. See the link in the previous footnote.

46. From part 2 of Cynthia's essay, "Motherhood: Autistic Parenting and Supports That Make a Difference." URL: http://autismwomensnetwork.org/motherhood-autistic-parenting-and-supports-that-make-a-difference/

47. From part 3, "Autistic Motherhood: Honoring Our Personal Choices." URL: http://autismwomensnetwork.org/autistic-motherhood-honoring-our-personal-choices/

Autism awareness knows nothing of the many mothers and fathers out there who are actually Autistic themselves. Because autism awareness is so entangled with a rhetoric of tragedy (and relies on maintaining the illusion that there are no such things as Autistic adults), the very idea of Autistic parents would be shocking: What if they passed their genetics on, creating more Autistic children?! From an autism awareness perspective, the thought is horrifying. But autism acceptance recognizes that there are already hundreds, probably thousands, of actually Autistic people quietly parenting, invisible to society, struggling and celebrating. It is time to move past awareness and accept the Autistic parents among us, offering encouragement and support. And listening to them. After all, as much as I do love and respect my friends who are non-autistic parents of Autistic children, who can you turn to for the truly insider view of raising Autistic children? Obviously Autistic parents of Autistic children. These are the parenting experts who understand and can explain how to nurture the autistic neurology – they literally know it inside and out.

L is for Love

Love. Those who say we have no empathy claim we are not capable of it, but we already established back at letter E that Autistic empathy doesn't always look just like non-autistic empathy, so who can marvel when I suggest that Autistic love has its own flavor as well?

If you doubt that we can love, know that the only thing that has sustained me sufficiently to write thousands of words of acceptance in a world that mainly speaks of us as hopeless burdens is love. Halfway through the month of April, the messages that chop away at my sense of self-worth are still everywhere I turn. I am still seeing a higher number of advertisements for Autism Speaks than I see the rest of the year, complete with the heart-rending tragedy language. Imagine that: a whole month each year is set aside to make everyone aware of what a burden you are and how much better the world will be when there are no longer people like you in it. What could sustain me through a month of seeing and hearing not only myself but scores of people I love being referred to like that? Love. I am writing because I love Autistic people and because I want to do what I can to increase acceptance. Yes, I promise you we can love. There are many days when love is the only thing that sustains us.

Beth Ryan writes of her Autistic daughter, "She lavishes love and affection on those close to her. She loves. She loves. She loves. Don't tell me she doesn't love. She LOVES. Think Autistic people are incapable of loving? That says more about you than it does about the people you're mis-characterizing."[48]

That is not even my favorite quote from Beth about love. She makes it abundantly clear that it is selfish to demand that Autistic people express love in ways identical to the ways non-autistic people express love when she writes, "I often hear things like, 'It is so sad that Autistic children can't tell their parents that they love them.' Actually, more often I hear parents say, 'I want my child to be able to tell me that he loves me.' When I think about Evie's communication, that's just about the furthest thing from my mind. I want to hear that her tummy hurts. I want to hear that she wants a glass of water. I want to hear that she is hungry. I want to hear the things that make her happy, scared, sad, angry, frustrated, tired. I mean 'hear' figuratively, not literally. I do not care if she speaks or points to a picture or clicks an icon on her iPad or types. I want communication for Evie. I want to stop guessing at what she needs and thinks so that I can answer her needs."[49]

Let that sink in for a moment. Could it be that the people who say that we Autistics don't know how to love . . . could it be that they are the ones who need more lessons in loving? Beth gets it. Beth sees that her daughter loves, and Beth sees that being there when her child needs her is more loving

48. From "ability to love: presume competence", on *Love Explosions*. URL:
    http://loveexplosions.net/2014/11/05/ability-to-love-presume-competence/
49. From "the words I want to hear," also on *Love Explosions*. URL:
    http://loveexplosions.net/2013/04/11/the-words-i-want-to-hear/

than wringing her hands because she has to see her daughter's love, as it is lived out in each moment of her life, instead of getting those three words from her child? And this is what autism acceptance looks like: It looks like Beth, seeing her daughter's love and caring more about meeting her daughter's needs than about getting verbal confirmation of what she already knows to the core of her being: that her daughter is filled with love.

Because we are. We are filled with love. See how K says it, "The way I love? It is deep. Autism is deep love. People write it off as special interest or obsession, but even if it's not something I can excel at, I can excel at loving what I love, loving what I do, loving who I love. Autism is being able to be consumed by love and interest, it is giving 100% because it is an insult to the thing one loves to give any less. Autism is going big or going home."[50]

I wish I could say that anyone who is loved by an Autistic person deeply knows that they are loved, but sadly I still see that some people are unsure of the love, even in the middle of receiving it. I've even watched video footage of more than one mother saying they just don't know if their child is even aware of them or knows who they are . . . while their child is clearly showing love toward their mother, that minute, while she is speaking, even in the middle of her doubts. It is a sad thing to see.

Do not doubt it. We do love!

Researchers doubt it. And they come up with strange theories about why we don't love. For example, some researchers depleted the oxytocin and serotonin in mice (in MICE!) and saw that they didn't want to socialize any more, so they said that we don't get neurochemical rewards from interacting with others.[51] Because some mice didn't like having the oxytocin and serotonin depleted in their brains? Seriously? Seriously??

"'People with autism-spectrum disorders may not experience the normal reward the rest of us all get from being with our friends,' the study's lead author, Dr. Robert Malenka, professor of psychiatry and behavioral sciences at Stanford University said in a statement, 'For them, social interactions can

---

50. From "What autism really is", on Radical Neurodivergence Speaking. URL:
    http://timetolisten.blogspot.com/2013/11/what-autism-really-is.html
51. URL: http://www.ncbi.nlm.nih.gov/pubmed/24025838

be downright painful.'"[52]

Yes, social interactions can be painful. But it has nothing to do with mice. And I'm pretty sure it has nothing to do with oxytocin. People sometimes smell funny. They are loud. They move quickly in unpredictable ways that raise my anxiety levels. They randomly touch me, often for no clear reason, and almost always without asking first. They make fun of me. They get angry. They say, "what the hell is wrong with you?" They say, "aw poor widdle baby is crying again!" And not in a comforting way; they laugh at me as they say it. They want to socialize in places with loud espresso machines. Or glaring fluorescent lights. They want to go to the mall and they laugh if they're told the mall is scary.

But scientists don't know any of this. They think they can learn more about how and whether we love by altering mice than by interacting with us. Now who was it, again, that finds interactions painful? Scientists: put down the mice and spend quality time with us! We do love. And even those of us who don't use our voices, even those of us who don't use words at all, can tell you more about love than your hormonally-challenged mice will.

M is for Murder

I have been dreading M. I don't want to write this chapter, but I have no choice. This is one of the most important letters in the autism acceptance alphabet because this is the very worst outcome of autism awareness without autism acceptance. This is the grim truth about what happens when we are portrayed as pointless burdens who crumble marriages, bankrupt families, and destroy the lives of everyone around us.

---

52. From "What the 'Love Hormone' Has to Do With Autism", *Time Magazine Online,* September 12, 2013. URL: http://healthland.time.com/2013/09/12/what-the-love-hormone-has-to-do-with-autism/

When parents learn about their child's diagnosis of autism and turn to others for help, they need hope and they need realism. They need to hear from people who have been parenting Autistic children, and they need to hear from those voices that, yes, it is hard. But all parenting is hard. They need to hear that all parenting also has joy and satisfaction and they need to hear that they will find that joy and satisfaction, too. They need to find a community that is supportive when parents need to vent about how difficult it is but also a community that does not condone hate speech toward innocent children.

Sadly, what too many parents find is a community filled with gloom and doom and endless complaint. They too often find themselves in a community of people who portray themselves as martyrs and victims and their beautiful children as abusers and punishments. Yes, I have heard parents describe their Autistic children as abusers because the parents do not understand and have not been taught how to help their child get their needs met. I'm sure you've heard parents say "I love my child, but I hate his autism." Well, I've been chilled to hear a parent actually say that they hated their child. Not autism; their child. That is what the parents getting support from martyrdom communities are encouraging in each other: a hatred of their precious children.

Some parents manage to rise above the negativity. In "What I Wish I'd Been Made Aware of When My Daughter Was Diagnosed With Autism," on *Emma's Hope Book*, Ariane writes, "Disregard any organization that describes autism and your child as tragic, an epidemic, a burden or any other word generally reserved for warfare. If you read or hear something that causes you to feel fear, walk away, it is most likely inaccurate and intended to make you afraid.   None of us are able to help our children when we are terrified. Fear can cause us to make decisions we will later regret."[53]

This is the voice of experience. Ariane is a strong ally to her Autistic daughter, Emma, and to the entire Autistic community, but she has written

---

53. URL: https://emmashopebook.com/2013/04/04/what-i-wish-id-been-made-aware-of-when-my-daughter-was-diagnosed-with-autism/

about the regrets she has over past beliefs that came from a place of fear. Emma's family was living in fear because their first exposure to autism consisted of doctors, organizations, and a community of parents who were also filled with fear instead of acceptance. Emma's parents, Ariane and Richard, were afraid, but they also saw so much joy and brilliance in their beloved daughter and when they finally met Autistic adults, they were eager to learn from us.

Emma's family are not the sort of people to get mired in feelings of victimhood. I know a little bit of the family's history and I have a huge amount of respect for everyone in the family– they have all been through so much, long before Emma was born, and they are strong survivors, deep thinkers, and well-educated. They are the kind of people who find their way out of shadows of fear. Too many other people get stuck in those shadows and their children suffer as a result.

Sometimes parents (or other guardians) are so frightened and stuck that they kill their children. The parents are so filled with despair and grief that they decide it would be better if their child were dead. Sometimes their despair warps their thoughts so much that they feel like killing their child is somehow saving them from a life of suffering. Sometimes those parents also try to commit suicide along with their child because they feel so much despair and depression that they believe that they should go with their child in death.[54] Some of these parents do succeed in their suicides, but most times, those suicide attempts are half-hearted and unsuccessful, mere gestures. Other parents are equally guilty of murder although they don't intentionally kill their children. Some parents kill their children accidentally through the application

---

54. Two recent, high profile cases of failed parental suicide after attempts to kill their child are the grisly murder of Alex Spourdalakis and the attempted murder of Issy Stapleton.

Alex: http://autisticadvocacy.org/2013/06/asan-calls-for-federal-hate-crime-prosecution-for-the-murder-of-alex-spourdalakis/

Issy: http://autisticadvocacy.org/2013/09/asan-statement-on-the-attempted-murder-of-issy-stapleton/

of brutal "treatments" such as chelation or bleach enemas.[55]

I'm hoping you're asking yourself right now how any parent could give their child a bleach enema. The answer? Fear. Love is stronger than fear, but fear can hide love too well for the power of love to take effect. A parent who is terrified of autism can allow that fear to overpower the love they have for their child. In a nauseatingly tragic act, echoing the fable in the Nathaniel Hawthorne short story, "The Birthmark,"[56] a parent can so desperately attempt to scrub away the autism that they destroy their own child, just as the scientist in Hawthorne's story thought he might perfect his young wife by removing the birthmark on her face but instead poisoned her.

Hawthorne writes that "he failed to look beyond the shadowy scope of time, and, living once for all in eternity, to find the perfect future in the present." This can be taken as an allegory for those parents who cannot love the child life placed in their care but rather must destroy that child with poisons they had hoped would magically transform them into the child they wished they had instead. Of course this is impossible– there is no "other child" lurking inside an Autistic child, waiting to be freed. A parent can love their child or reject their child but autism cannot be bleached out of them; it is at the core of who their child is.

The reason I am writing about autism acceptance– the reason our whole community is making such a lot of noise about acceptance– is because awareness without acceptance is deadly. Literally deadly. Awareness without acceptance is fear. Fear of autism hurts Autistics. A culture of fear leads to murder. We haven't got complete records of how many Autistics get killed by their parents or caretakers, but the 2015 Day of Mourning[57] vigil website

---

55. Killed by chelation: http://www.medpagetoday.com/neurology/autism/1616

   Killed by bleach: http://www.bbc.com/news/uk-england-london-11758290

   See also: http://www.forbes.com/sites/emilywillingham/2013/10/29/the-5-scariest-autism-treatments/#72a7134c5fc7

56. Archival PDF URL:
   http://www.lem.seed.pr.gov.br/arquivos/File/livrosliteraturaingles/birthmark.pdf

57. URL: http://autisticadvocacy.org/2015/02/2015-day-of-mourning-vigil-sites/

says that over 70 people with disabilities have been murdered by their parents or caretakers in the last 5 years. That's more than one per month.

The first murdered Autistic I became aware of was Marcus Fiesel, killed at age 4 in 2006. Marcus loved flowers and Bob the Builder. Everyone who knew him said he was a sweet and lovable boy. His mother was having a hard time keeping the household together, so Marcus was in foster care. His foster parents wanted to go out of town so they put tape on Marcus's mouth and wrists and rolled him up in a carpet and locked him in a closet while they left town for the weekend. Marcus died from overheating and suffocation.[58]

As devastating and depressing as it was to read about the murder of Marcus Fiesel, in the decade since then I have watched person after person murdered. It is easy for me to believe that the killings happen more often than once a month because I see the news stories every month, sometimes two in a month. There are a few isolated killings that get a strong public reaction of outrage toward the killer– the most recent was when London McCabe's mother threw him off a bridge to drown. But more often, the reaction I see in the comments under news stories are horrifying to me.

People defend the killers. They say that it is "understandable" that they "snapped" because we are such "burdens." The ableism is thick and I have learned to avert my eyes from the comment sections under these news stories because it is so angering and distressing to see so many people justifying the murder of people like me.

Emily Willingham wrote, "It's become typical, again and again, for parents who murder their autistic children to get some kind of a 'pass' from the commentariat and the news media because, well, 'autism is such a challenge.' That's in part because some autism organizations and members of the news media have successfully presented autism as a 'monster' and a 'kidnapper' instead of as the developmental condition that it is. So in the public mind, an allegedly overwhelmed mother with 'no supports' should

58. Case background via Wikipedia. URL: https://en.wikipedia.org/wiki/Marcus_Fiesel

certainly be pitied and not judged harshly for killing the 'monster.'"[59]

Shannon Des Rocha Rosa wrote, "Our autistic children's lives are no less valuable than other children's lives. But they are often harder, especially when parents focus on normalizing or curing autism, rather than supporting and understanding children who depend on them. [...] We need to, must do better by our autistic children. We must do our best to support and understand them and their autism, and stop torturing them by trying to turn them into the non-autistic child they will never be. Specifically, if you cannot accept your child's autism for their sake, then please– do it so your role as a parent will be easier. If that's what it takes to stop someone from killing their autistic child, so be it."[60]

Michelle Sutton wrote, "The reason people feel sorry for me when they find out my kids are autistic is that they don't know anything about autism except that it makes them hard to live with. They know this because the media tells them.

"And this is what I'm talking about when I say 'autism awareness' doesn't help autistic people, and that the media has no place blaming autistic children for their own murders.

"So instead of listening to the facts being spoken by autistic people and their allies, people listen to the media tell them that autistic people are violent and difficult to live with. So society moves down the slippery slope of assumption until it reaches the point where vilifying children based on a diagnosis is acceptable."[61]

And this is why we need autism acceptance. Autism awareness kills. Autism awareness stigmatizes. Autism awareness blames Autistic people for the crimes others commit against us.

Autism acceptance welcomes us to be part of the big human family:

---

59. From "If a Parent Murders an Autistic Child, Who Is to Blame?" Forbes Online. URL: http://www.forbes.com/sites/emilywillingham/2013/09/05/if-a-parent-murders-an-autistic-child-who-is-to-blame/

60. From "We Cannot Excuse Parents Who Kill Autistic Children" on BlogHer. URL: http://www.blogher.com/we-cannot-excuse-parents-who-kill-autistic-children

61. From "Autism, Stigma and Murder." Huffington Post. URL: http://www.huffingtonpost.com/michelle-sutton/autism-stigma-and-murder_b_5211817.html

Respected, valued, protected.

We need to build a world where parents learning about their child's diagnosis are welcomed into a community of love and support, not of fear. We need to build a world where a huge organization cannot vacuum up all the available donation money by telling us that Autistic children are "like lepers" and their parents are "like Saint Francis of Assisi." We need to build a world where it is unthinkable for people to side with a murderer and blame their victim for being such a "horrible burden" that killing them was "understandable."

We need to build a world of autism acceptance.

N is for No Means No

As adults we talk about things like rape prevention, and we use the slogan "No Means No." That is to say, respecting someone else's "no," at any time, for any reason, is the rational, adult, ethical thing to do. There are a lot of strong and powerful words being put out about respecting other people's boundaries and autonomy.

A strange thing about "No Means No" is that it only applies to adults. The more vulnerable members of our society– children– are rarely allowed to own their "no.' And then somehow we expect them to morph overnight from people who have spent nearly two decades having their boundaries violated by people more powerful than them (adults) to people who are eager to respect other people's boundaries, even the boundaries of those who are weaker than them (often women, thus the rape prevention connection of this slogan).

And, for the moment here, I am not talking about just Autistic children. This is something we do to all children, regardless of neurology. Now, you're probably saying that sometimes children need to have their boundaries violated and I will not argue that with you. For example, we have to teach children that there are big, fast-moving, deadly cars to pay attention to and not run in front of. This is a perennial facet of parenting– in other generations there were Roman soldiers to not piss off or hungry saber-toothed tigers and dire wolves to not look like lunch in front of.

Another example is life-saving/changing medical treatment. Kids don't want surgery or chemotherapy or orthodontic braces, but parents who choose their child's health over their boundaries are making a loving choice. Hopefully, there is lots of talking about outcomes and the boundaries are violated in as gentle and informed a way as possible. There are some boundaries in childhood that are pretty much inevitably going to get dismissed for a particular life-and-death sort of purpose and that's okay. Difficult for everyone involved, but okay. I am very happy that my parents pushed me into getting my teeth aligned by discussing the results with me and offering encouragement and support to continue when the procedures became more painful.

Still, there are thousands of minor boundary transgressions made against children all the time. For example, my father– who, I should mention, loves me dearly and was a wonderful daddy– used to answer my request for a chocolate bar by saying, "you don't want a chocolate bar." Not "I am not going to buy you a chocolate bar," or "I don't have the money for a chocolate bar," or "I want to see you eat something healthier, so I'm not getting you a chocolate bar," or "chocolate is for birthdays, Christmas, and Easter, so you'll just have to wait for the next holiday." No, he told me I didn't <u>want</u> a chocolate bar. This was very confusing to me– I had thought I wanted a chocolate bar. I still felt very much like I wanted a chocolate bar, despite being told I didn't. Were my wants true? It was baffling to me and a minor boundary transgression (telling me I didn't feel the way it was obvious that I did feel) that subtly chipped away at my sense of self and autonomy.

I'm a very concrete thinker. It never occurred to me that "you don't want that" was just an expression of speech for my father. It was something far less subtle to me. Wanting a chocolate bar and not getting it was bad enough. Being told that I didn't even know myself well enough to understand what I wanted was diminishing in ways I'm only now beginning to understand, decades later. Small statements have big consequences, especially when you stack a mountain of thousands of small statements day after day, but even these sorts of boundary transgressions are minor compared to the level of compliance that is so often expected from Autistic children. Too often, in the name of therapy or early intervention, Autistic children are subject to a systematic demolishing of their sense of autonomy and their right to say "no" and be heard. If non-autistic children were treated the way Autistic children are, most people would be horrified.

"Touch your nose."

"Touch your nose."

"Touch your nose." The therapist takes the child's hand and forces it to the child's nose while saying once again, "touch your nose." Then, "good girl! Here's a gummy bear!" A pause, then, "touch your nose."

"Touch your nose."

"Touch your nose."

It is a technique I have seen used to train bears to do tricks. It is a method used to train dogs and horses to perform on command. It is a common behavioral modification program for Autistic children. Please tell me you see something wrong with training Autistic children as if they are animals, using techniques reserved only for disabled children– techniques that would shock most people if they were used on non-disabled children.

Now, there's nothing inherently wrong with asking someone to touch their nose. I am ten years older than my sister and when she was a little toddler, one of our favorite games was for me (or Mom) to say, "where are your ears?" She would grin and touch them. "Where is your nose?" Again, a smile and a touch. We'd go through all the objects– her toes, her teddy bear, the blue ball, the red ball. She didn't need gummy bears because she loved the game and the attention. She was eager to show off that she knew all these things. But even if she needed an incentive to show us things, that's still not horrible. There's nothing inherently wrong with giving someone candy or stickers for showing that they know the letter S or where their nose is.

Where the touch nose sort of training goes horribly wrong is when we forget that No Means No. Autistic children don't have as many resources for saying no, so they say it in ways that get labeled as "non-compliance." They turn their head away. They get up from the table and walk away (or try to!) They cry. They scream. They hit. They bite.

And then they get labeled: Violent and non-compliant.

But what were those children supposed to do? No means no, right? For everybody, right? Or maybe only for non-autistic adults? Children don't get to say no? Children who can't shape the sounds of "no" with their mouths don't get to say no?

There are people who say that "touch your nose and get a gummy bear" is very important. There are people who say that a child must go through hundreds of repetitions of touching their nose or they will never have a chance in life. There are people who say a child must spend 40 hours a week sitting at that table, touching their nose over and over. And there are people who say that the cries and hitting are just "manipulation" and should be ignored. The protests have to be worked through and the nose has to be touched. And touched. And touched.

How is it manipulation to try to assert one's self? How is using any method available to say "no" a manipulation? How can I hear people saying these things and not think of "no means no" and how grossly it's being violated?

Sexual abuse is high among those of us with intellectual or developmental disabilities. The Arc reports several studies that found frighteningly high rates of sexual abuse against children and adults with intellectual disabilities, ranging from 1/4 to 1/2 of disabled people being the target of serious abuse.[62] A study published in the journal Child Abuse and Neglect found that nearly 1/5 of Autistic children had been abused sexually or physically.[63] This is not a population that should be taught that their no doesn't mean no. This is the population that *most* needs to be taught to own their no, defend their boundaries.

Look at it this way: is it better to push and push a child, while ignoring their boundaries and attempts to say no, so that they can perform a task on

62. URL: http://www.thearc.org/page.aspx?pid=2457
63. URL: http://www.ncbi.nlm.nih.gov/pubmed/1629330

command but are primed for victimization? I, and many of my friends and colleagues, believe it is better to respect a child's personal, individual learning time table. A strong sense of self is so important when it comes to protecting one's self and refusing to allow others to violate one's boundaries. Respecting a child's boundaries and limits may result in a child who reaches "developmental milestones" later than their age peers, but that child will arrive with intact boundaries and less likelihood of falling prey to predators and abusers.

I see a lot of parents struggling hard to make their child "indistinguishable from his peers" or "school ready" at the "right" age. It is worthy to want to help your child. It is important to work to help your child achieve her full potential. But also, it is crucial to teach your child to say no– with whatever voice your child is able to use– and be heard. It is vital to respect your child's autonomy and not sacrifice their safety for your learning goals.

Children develop. Even children with developmental disabilities develop– just on our own schedules and in our own ways. A study of children who were not speaking by age 4 found that nearly half of them spoke fluently as adults. When you add in the adults who were not speaking fluently but could communicate well using short phrases, the number of non-speaking children who grew up to be speaking adults went up to 70%.[64]

"But that won't be my child!" I've heard parents retort. "The definition of autism has been broadened too far. Those children are high-functioning. They aren't like my child! My child has REAL autism! My child has Kanner's autism, not Asperger's!"

The first person ever diagnosed with autism by Dr. Kanner drives a car and plays golf today.

Oh, he's still Autistic. Read the biographical article about him published in *The Atlantic*, "Autism's First Child,"[65] and you'll see that he's very Autistic. But he lives in a community with lots of support and accommodations. And love. Donald Triplett is very loved and respected in his community.

Forget "indistinguishable from peers" and focus on building a world of Triplett-friendly communities. Stop interpreting outbursts as "emotional

64. URL: http://pediatrics.aappublications.org/content/131/4/e1128
65. URL: http://www.theatlantic.com/magazine/archive/2010/10/autisms-first-child/308227/

manipulation" and start looking for the root causes. And teach your children– all your children– what boundaries are and how to say "no" and make it stick.

No means no. That is a basic truth of a respectful society. Do not teach your child that they are outsiders to that social contract. Thoreau taught it, Martin Luther King Jr. taught it, and you can teach it: when demands for compliance become unreasonable, it is a fundamental human right to say "no."

O is for Overloaded, Overstimulated, and Overwhelmed

There are several types of experiences that tend to make Autistic folks overloaded, overstimulated, or overwhelmed. As with most things, it's different from person to person. Some people might respond to one of the triggers discussed below; others respond to all of them. Some might seem pretty solid most of the time, others might always be living so close to the anxious edge that it does not take very much at all to push them over. Many of us are both of these extremes, at different times and in different situations.

That's an important thing to remember: When you're talking about things like "severity" or "functioning levels", it's better to just step back and not use that framework at all and instead talk in terms of support needs. We all have support needs and the amount and type of support we need can change from day to day, throughout the day, from minute to minute, from year to year. We are dynamic, not static, and how much support we need, how overloaded we become, how we react to the stresses of life– these things are constantly changing. Over time, we develop coping abilities, develop new skills, grow up, gain perspective. In the moment, we find or put ourselves into environments with more or less stimulation, have unexpected encounters with other people, weather, animals, the sharp corners of furniture. Life is always changing and we are always changing along with it.

I don't always know how much input I can handle. Think about that for a minute. I'm almost 50 years old. I've had decades of life in this body and brain. I've carefully studied life and my responses to it. And I still am not always sure whether I can handle something or not. Sometimes, a thing I could handle yesterday is out of my grasp today. Sometimes, a place that is usually good for me is very hard to cope with. Sometimes I'm not even sure what is stressing me out. Sometimes I'm not very good at even realizing I'm stressed out at all and in need of a break. If I, a middle-aged adult, do not always know when I need to take a break, how much more must you be compassionate with a child who has not learned as many self-regulation skills yet?

The main triggers I have noticed in myself and others (which is to say these are not necessarily the only triggers of overload, just some of the more common ones) are sensory input, emotions (our own and others'), and demands exceeding our executive function abilities.

Sensory input was the one that most recently did me in. I am on a limited data plan when it comes to the internet, and my writing process involves being online, pulling up links to include, looking up data to get facts correct, and even popping back and forth between writing and other activities on days when I need to break what I'm doing into pieces. My data plan re-sets mid month and I was low on data so I decided to go out to WiFi spots to write.

Normally, I have little trouble working in public. I have a few favorite WiFi spots, including a nice, quiet little independently-owned coffee shop. What I had forgotten was that it was Friday night. I keep a non-traditional schedule, so "weekend" doesn't have a lot of personal meaning. I work every day, except when I need to rest. I don't use a calendar to tell me when to work or rest because it is healthier for me to listen to my body's cues. The personal rule of listening to my body works with the main exception of those times when I am so intent on doing something that I inadvertently over-ride my body's cues, not noticing how much it is screaming for something until it is screaming so loudly I am breaking apart. That's what happened to me on Friday.

I started out in the coffee house and things were going fine until a large group of loud and high-pitched shrieking people sat right next to me. I put on headphones and started streaming Vivaldi, but the loud shrieks cut through everything and they HURT. I have a condition called vestibular hyperacusis which can best be described as a sort of synaesthesia that translates sound into motion. The more common form of hyperacusis, cochlear hyperacusis, translates certain sounds into pain. Vestibular hyperacusis is pain plus dizziness, disorientation, nausea, etc. When I hear certain high-pitched sounds, it feels as if the floor is sliding away from under me. It's like being sea sick. And it's pretty horrible.

Next, some musicians decided to play. Normally, that's a good thing. I've often been very pleasantly entertained by impromptu, amateur jam sessions. I like that. It is utterly delightful to me. That is not what was happening on that Friday, though. Four people picked up instruments and started playing four different songs, each getting louder and louder, trying to out-play the other three. It was a horrible cacophony. I turned up the volume on Vivaldi but still couldn't quite drown the noise out.

But I was stubbornly trying to finish writing an essay and I tried to just "power through it." This is a bad idea. And I know, partly, where it comes from. All my life, I've had people say, "it's not that bad", "just tough it out and you will get used to it," "stop acting like such a baby!" I've internalized a lot of the shame and so when I should have just packed things up and gone home, I tried to power through the stress and suffering instead. I stayed until the coffee house closed and I got a lot of work done, despite the pain.

But I wasn't finished. I should have just gone home, but instead I went to a 24-hour McDonald's (still unaware that it was Friday night) to try to finish. A busload of pre-teens came in, hyper from some activity, and started playing Ping-Pong across the restaurant. Again, the noise was horrible, and now I had balls whizzing past me, inches from my face. I stubbornly kept writing, finished my work, and went home.

I slept for days. I slept all of Saturday and most of Sunday. Monday afternoon, I woke up long enough to re-schedule an appointment to Tuesday. Tuesday I made the appointment but spent the rest of the day before and after sleeping. On Wednesday I slept twelve hours and awoke, finally feeling "right" enough to accomplish things again. Spending Friday evening fighting against excessive and overloading sensory input because I wanted to finish what I was doing cost me about four days of . . . . of life, really. Not just four days of work but four days of everything. This is why "just tough it out" is such a bad idea. If I had listened to my body and listened to the advice I am always giving to other people, I would have gone home (or noticed it was Friday and not gone out in the first place). I stubbornly wanted to get some work done but by trying to force my way through it, I lost several days of productivity.

The root of the problem was that I was not treating myself the way I ask people to treat the Autistics in their lives. I should have removed myself from the stress, but I didn't. Pay attention to sensory input and how it might be stressing out the Autistic people in your life (including yourself). The grocery store is a really common place for meltdowns and it's easy to see why: Flickering fluorescent lights, bright colors shouting in chaotic ways, words everywhere you look, (other) children crying, people milling around (visual motion is one of my sensory sensitivities and it makes it hard to be in a crowded place because not only are there sounds and smells and touches but everything around me is moving in unpredictable ways!), painful and garbled announcements on overhead speakers, and in the warehouse groceries there is echoing sound and the shrill beeping of forklifts backing up. Is it any surprise that the grocery store is one of the biggest challenges for Autistic people as well as for the mothers of young Autistics? It's a place we usually have to go if we want to eat but can be a sensory nightmare to be there.

Emotions are overloading and overwhelming. I laughed at my great-grandmother's funeral and it (understandably) made people in my family very upset, but I loved Grandma Mary deeply. She was my favorite family member. She was the one who always accepted me, even when no one else could. She taught me what unconditional love looks like. I loved her so much that I'm feeling very emotional right now, just remembering her and feeling the loss. Just about every day of my life, I wish she were still alive. But I laughed at her funeral because I was so emotionally overloaded and overwhelmed.

My cousin did her best to rescue me. She grabbed my hand and dragged me away saying, "Excuse us, she's really choked up!" to try to cover the giggles I was struggling to suppress. She pulled me after her into the bathroom and let me laugh in private. Laughter is contagious, and so pretty soon she was laughing along with me, even though I know she deeply loved Grandma Mary, too. I am so grateful to my cousin for pulling me out of that situation– I rarely get such beautiful and compassionate support. And I am consoled by the knowledge that Grandma Mary would have loved and accepted me, even seeing me laugh at her funeral. She was always on my side and she knew I loved her. I wish I hadn't upset my family so much. But I guess by that point they were used to seeing just about anything from me and just added it to the tally of strangeness.

Another emotionally overwhelming situation was when I tried to get lunch in the food court at my university during finals week. I had an exam coming up in 90 minutes and figured I ought to put food in me first. So I already had a huge stress overload as anyone who has ever survived a finals week would know. I went to a food vendor and asked for "Fire and Rice," a favorite meal. I mentioned that I wanted the sriracha added during cooking, not after, because it tasted better that way. The cook said okay. Still, I watched him with an eagle eye because I had lots of experience with my food not being prepared the way I asked. He did not add sriracha. He quickly scooped everything into a bowl and I said, "you didn't add sriracha."

He said, "I can put some in now if you want."

I said, "it's better when it's added during cooking."

He said, "I did add it. You weren't watching."

I was confronted with a dilemma. I was sure he hadn't added it because I was carefully watching for him to. But what if he did add it and I had somehow missed seeing it and asked him to put more and then the food was overseasoned and unpleasant to eat with no time left to cook more before my exam? Was he lying to me? I hate being lied to! Was he playing me for a fool? Had he really done something while I was watching for him to do it and I didn't see?

I didn't know what to do and I lost control. I figure the people seeing me melt down figured I was some kind of spoiled brat. Or maybe they were used to seeing this kind of behavior during finals week? I started to leave and a woman approached me timidly, as if she were frightened of me, trying to calm me down and get my needs met. I ended up running away to a hiding place in the bathroom where I sobbed and hit myself for an hour until I was calm enough to go take my exam.

It's a small thing, someone made my food wrong and possibly lied to me about it, but it was too much emotion on top of the high level of emotion I was already walking around with. (Everyone around me was stressed and emotional because of finals week and I am like a sponge, soaking in other people's emotions as well. One thing I love about my best friend is how calm he remains in the face of just about anything. I tease him about it sometimes, but in truth I love his stoic nature because it is so much easier for me to remain calm when the people around me are calm.)

Some ways to try to mitigate emotional overload include staying calm around the Autistic people you care for, even during a meltdown, and helping the Autistic children in your life to learn to identify and name their own emotions. I know, it's not easy. But the less you react emotionally to an Autistic person's emotional distress, the easier it will be for them to recover from emotional overstimulation. I find that the more I am able to recognize my emotional states, the better I am at calming myself and, if needed and possible, removing myself from emotionally stressful situations. It's still not easy for me. It's a work in progress. I will probably be working on self-regulation skills for the rest of my life.

Executive function overload is also pretty common. One thing I've noticed that sets other people off but I seem to handle reasonably well (although I do it much more slowly than I observe non-Autistic people doing it) is filling out forms. I have watched people completely disintegrate over a job application or a medical form. I do understand and relate to it–

someone who knows what should be put in the form boxes and who can read and write just falls apart at putting all that together. There's a . . . stuckness. It's part of why I am slow at filling out forms (dysgraphia– difficulty with handwriting– is the other part of why forms are extra tedious for me). If someone you know has a hard time with forms, don't shame them. Don't tell them to suck it up because they have to learn some day. Help them! Help them with the form and, if you can, along the way talk about what you are doing to help them learn form-management skills.

Another overwhelming, executive-function related experience is housework and self-care. Every day, we are supposed to shower, brush our teeth, style our hair, feed ourselves, clean our homes. It is overwhelming because there are so many tasks with so many steps, and if they go undone, there are even more tasks; it piles up. The worse things get, the harder it is to start doing something about them. I keep checklists, broken down into the smallest bites, and it helps. But the moment things get away from me, the checklists don't work anymore. When things get too chaotic, you can't fix thing A because thing B is in the way but you can't fix thing B because thing A is in the way. The result is overwhelm, overload, breakdown.

Where it can get confusing is that the reactions to overload can be so different. Crying, meltdown, anger, self-injury, shutdown, long sleeps, overeating, undereating. Almost any kind of stress reaction you can imagine and some that never occurred to you. What makes it harder? The biggest challenge for me is when people blame me or mock me for struggling to cope. I've been told, "you just *want* to be upset." No. No, I don't. I don't want to be upset at all. Being upset is horrible and stressful and exhausting. Being upset is what happens when a limit gets reached and I can't pull back from the edge any more. Just like a person who needs to vomit and is stuck in public has no choice but to vomit in front of everyone, an Autistic who has reached overload and is stuck in public has no choice but to stress out in front of everyone.

It's embarrassing. Humiliating. Traumatic. I never went back to that food court the rest of the time I was a student at that university. I couldn't bear to revisit the scene of my trauma, the place of my shame. The loss of control is frightening. The loss of dignity is appalling. When a person pushes me to overload, especially when they over-ride my protests to do so, I experience a massive loss of trust and disassociate myself from that person. When someone tells you that they can't handle something, your instinct may be to be a cheerleader and push them into it. "Of course you can! I'll be right by your side the whole time!" "Don't limit yourself with can't!" "The only disability is a bad attitude!" There are all kinds of cheery platitudes meant to push people past their comfort zone. Sometimes that comfort zone is there for a very real reason and it's important to respect that. Don't lead with "Of course you can!" Lead with, "Can you tell me what makes it hard for you?"

Psychologists often get it all wrong. They try to apply psychology to episodes of overwhelm and meltdowns when what is primarily occurring is neurology. Yes, a psychological component can develop– going through multiple stressful breakdowns will leave a psychological mark on a person– but overload, overstimulation, overwhelm, meltdown, shutdown are manifestations of neurology, of having a nervous system that is wired differently and has a pattern of over-sensitivities and under-sensitivities that diverge from the expected. In saying this, I don't intend to present a neurology/psychology schism, because it's all connected. I just want you to understand that two people who are doing what looks like the exact same thing can be doing it for two completely different reasons, so it's important not to assume that you know what's going on with a person, especially if your assumption is that an Autistic person in distress is just "spoiled" or needs counseling.

Psychologists are trained to be alarmed by "self-isolation." They often see a patient who presents with symptoms of depression, whether actual or misread. Sometimes our normal ways of being look like depression when they are not. Sometimes our depression does not look like depression. We talked about this before, back in Chapter D. The professional believes that the apparent depression is caused by the self-isolation so they urge the person to get out more, "put yourself out there," to be more socially active. The problem with this is that some of us have chosen self-isolation because we are trying to avoid overload, overstimulation, and overwhelm. I love people. I think I may actually be a hidden extrovert– hidden by my tendency toward sensory overload. I can't "put myself out there" more than I do. Paradoxically, when I try to follow that sort of advice from a therapist, I become *more* depressed as a result.

It's okay to help us find our limits if we don't know what they are. It's okay to help us grow past our limits in manageable bites that leave us in sufficient control, but it is imperative to respect our limits when we communicate them to you. We live in these bodies and we learn, over time, how much they can handle. If the amount we can cope with is less than you think is normal or acceptable, it is not your job to try to force us "out of our shells." We aren't in shells. Often, we are simply practicing self-care. Respect that. Do not force us and do not shame us for having different limits than others. This is a very basic aspect of autism acceptance: accept our limits and follow *our* lead in moving past them. We live in a culture that teaches "no limits," but there really are limits. If you would not expect a person born into a body without a uterus to become impregnated and carry a child in their non-existent womb, if you would not expect a human body to sprout wings and fly away, then you understand that there really are limits. Don't ridicule or pressure others whose limits are not what you think they should be.

Help us to grow in ways that don't cause us to fling ourselves to the floor or fall limply passive or scream and hurt ourselves. Help us to grow in ways that are not stressful and damaging. Research has shown that repeated stressful stimulation changes the brain in damaging ways. This means that pushing and pressuring us repeatedly to the point of meltdown or shutdown can permanently harm us. Do not damage us. Help us to find the ways to stay calm and focused. Help us to test our limits gently and with self-compassion. Respect us and do not seek to overload us– it is not the way to help us grow. "Get over it" should never be your motto for Autistic people. Please, help us learn to protect ourselves and respect our "no." Slow down. Listen to us. It may be horrible for you to have to be around us when we are overloaded, overstimulated, and overwhelmed, but I assure you it is infinitely more horrible for us to experience being in overload, overstimulation and overwhelm. Don't be angry. Don't blame us. Have compassion for our struggles and respect for everything we do to help ourselves.

P is for Poverty

I've (mostly) come to terms with my own poverty, but I worry about many of my fellow Autistic adults who are (often quite literally) starving and I worry about the children – what, if anything, will be there for them when they grow up?

Autism and poverty – well, disability of all types and poverty, actually – go hand in hand. That is not to say that every Autistic adult or every disabled adult lives in poverty, but a large percentage of us do. At a time when poverty and unemployment are declining among the general population, both are on the rise among the disabled population. The U.S. Census Bureau reported that in 2013 the U.S. poverty rate fell to 14.5% but the poverty rate for disabled people rose to 28.8 percent. The overall unemployment rate dropped to 6% but for disabled people it was over twice as high, at 12.8%. Seventy percent of the general U.S. population over the age of 16 are participating in the workforce while only 20% of the disabled population over age 16 are participating. Bear in mind that "disabled people over the age of 16" is a category comprising some 29 million people– 9% of the total U.S. population. No one knows how many Autistic people there are in the United States, but a reasonable estimate (based on the 1-in-68 statistic) is 4.6 million, roughly 3.5 million of whom would be over the age of 18 (based on the current age skew of the general U.S. population.[66])

For those three and a half million American Autistic adults, as well as their counterparts world-wide, the statistics are even more harsh.

Transitioning is more difficult for Autistic young adults than young adults with other disabilities. The National Longitudinal Transition Study-2 found that, when comparing adults aged 21 to 25, only 17% of Autistic young adults have lived independently, compared to 34% of young adults

---

66. URL: http://www.census.gov/population/age

with intellectual disability.[67]

In the UK, The National Autistic Society (NAS) reports that only 15% of Autistic adults are employed full-time and as many as one-third of adult Autistics have neither employment nor access to benefits.[68] The Simons Foundation Autism Research Initiative (SFARI) reports on Norwegian studies that find "mildly affected" (SFARI appears to dislike that phrase as much as I do) Autistic people having just as much difficulty with employment as people elsewhere on the autism spectrum.[69]

Shattuck and his team did a literature review[70] of services for adults on the autism spectrum and found (not surprisingly) a meager amount of data available. Job support was rated highly as "evidence-based," but I was concerned about the strong emphasis on training Autistic adults to perform as costume mascots in front of retail stores. It's a valid job, yes, and I've met some people who do seem to love it. But isn't there anything else for Autistic adults? Even those with university degrees too often remain unemployed or work part-time and cannot support themselves on their income.

When efforts are made to help us get higher-paying jobs, often everything seems to be centered around computer work. I've listened to many of my fellow Autistics complain that job assistance keeps pushing them toward computer and tech jobs despite their dyscalculia or other learning disabilities that make them unsuited for math and tech work. Moreover, many people do not realize that the computer industry has shifted over the course of the last twenty years or so. There was a time when computer work was a great choice for the socially disabled because there was a high need for skilled workers and few people with the skills to fill those jobs. Workers lacking in social skills were able to land secure, high-paying employment despite going down socially worse than a lead balloon in job interviews.

That time has passed. So many people train for the computer industries

67. URL http://aut.sagepub.com/content/18/5/562
68. URL: http://www.aspie-editorial.com/2011/01/22/employment-nas-dont-write-me-off-campaignautistic-people-condemned-to-poverty/
69. URL: https://spectrumnews.org/news/people-with-milder-forms-of-autism-struggle-as-adults/
70. URL: http://www.ncbi.nlm.nih.gov/pmc/articles/PMC3538849/

these days that competition for positions is high and jobs primarily go to those who are socially competent, who interview well, who have strong people skills. Still, the mythology lingers– have no social skills? Go work with computers! It's a damaging mythology because it can lead people to feel they don't need to work on interview skills or office socio-political competence because their tech skills will carry the day. And career counselors still try to funnel Autistic people into the computer industry without realizing that many of us will need just as much workplace support there as in any other occupation. They often do this without realizing that a significant portion of employable Autistics are more suited for work that uses other skills with words, images, music, animals, etc.

I read a very interesting paper written by two Autistic people, Rachel Silverman and James Williams, "Two Autistic Perspectives on the Workforce: An Undiagnosed Ivy League Graduate and a Male Author and Presenter with Autism," published on Williams' web site. The paper is about employment and self-sufficiency issues and one of their suggestions was to join the "autism industry": "First, they develop a book, artwork, jewelry, photography, or other salable product. Then they can rent space as exhibitors at autism and disability conferences for free or low cost. They can sell their products at these conferences and earn income in this fashion."

This is an intriguing concept, especially to an autism author like myself. I am wondering where all those "free or low cost" conference opportunities are, though. Every time one of my Autistic colleagues is invited to present at a disability or autism conference, they have to organize a fundraising campaign to try to get the money together to attend. Is the "autism industry" an option for talented, underemployed Autistics if the cost of attending conferences is a nearly insurmountable barrier?

The biggest question about the viability of this work model is this: is there room for two million workers in the "autism industry"? I honestly don't know. Maybe. Probably not. Professionals rarely listen to us, though increasing numbers of parents are thirsty for our perspective. I do encourage all Autistics to make their voice heard (or seen – all communication styles included!) because a richer, fuller understanding of autism depends on a rich, full number of Autistic voices fostering that understanding in all its complexity and diversity.

But can all Autistics (or even most) make a living sharing their words, art, jewelry, music, photographs, and so on, seeking to tap in to the "autism industry" as their sole method of marketing? It seems unlikely. Dr. Temple Grandin leans in the other direction, advising people not to become "professional autistics," but rather to follow her footsteps of holding a "real job" and advocating for autistics on the side. If only we could all achieve her level of professional success, but the employment statistics tell a different story.

Another valuable point in the paper by Silverman and Williams is that so much energy is going toward making Autistics employable and very little is going toward helping Autistics secure disability benefits. I understand the huge emotional investment in wanting to help us all get jobs, and I don't want to cut back on those efforts at all. It is very important to help Autistic people get and keep employment. But Silverman and Williams point out that we aren't all employable. Some of us have energy levels too low to sustain full-time employment. Some have health issues severe enough to result in a large number of missed work days. Additionally, many of our health needs (for example, special diets for people with celiac, a condition that occurs more frequently in the Autistic population than the general population) are expensive enough that a living wage for a non-disabled person is not a living wage for some of us.

When the data indicates that a third of Autistic adults have no job and no disability benefits, it is clear that an unacceptable number of us are falling through the cracks, and those "cracks" are actually gaping chasms. I feel very strongly that there should be more assistance for Autistic adults who need disability benefits but are having a hard time with the paperwork and documentation. Additionally, homelessness makes it harder to get disability benefits. I applied for SSI[71] several times before I finally got it– not because I was being turned down, but because I was too homeless and struggling to keep up with the application process. I'd get an address, apply, lose the

---

71. A U.S. disability welfare benefits for those who have not worked enough to get the income-based SSDI, a federal insurance program for disability.

address and be too busy trying to keep myself fed and safe to even think about how to follow up on the application and so it would lapse. When I finally got enough stability to follow through on the process, I was awarded SSI in less than 2 months from initial application– apparently, my case was what one might call a "shoo in." But when I couldn't keep a mailing address for two months, even a case as straightforward as mine was stymied.

Helping Autistic adults to get disability benefits isn't glamorous. It is hard to feel like one is doing good work when the focus has always been so strongly directed toward getting disabled people into the workforce. I think there should still be a strong focus on supporting Autistic people in employment goals, but it's clear that it's time to admit that some Autistics– even some highly educated Autistics– are not going to be able to work. We need more legitimate work-at-home opportunities, more support and assistance in finding and keeping online employment, a more individualized approach to vocational assistance, and a lot of help in getting disability benefits for those who aren't able to work full-time or at all. We live in a political climate where poor people are blamed for their poverty and disabled people, particularly those without obvious physical disabilities, are viewed with great skepticism, so vulnerable people who really need disability benefits should get help with the often confusing process of application, appeals, documentation, and more.

I spent a lot of time living in the streets and eating at soup kitchens and from dumpsters before I was able to get on SSI. I want people to understand how easy it is for Autistic adults to end up homeless. I've also had plenty of Autistic friends who were living in sub-standard conditions– for example, without running water or heat. I've been in that position myself, too. Our poverty levels are more than twice those of the general population and we are a very vulnerable population, comprised of many people who do not know how to ask for help with homework or cooking, let alone help with income, housing, healthcare, and survival. There needs to be more autism-accepting, non-judgmental assistance we can turn to. There need to be people trained in helping us get and keep employment and helping us get disability benefits. Too many of us are homeless, hungry, and without adequate medical care (both due to the barriers described earlier in chapter H is for Healthcare Access and due to the economic barriers that still exist, even after the passage of the Affordable Care Act in the United States and the existence of universal healthcare in other places such as the UK and Canada).

Yes, some of us are doing very well. But we aren't all Silicon Valley workers. We aren't all Temple Grandin or John Elder Robison. And many of us are living with aging parents who don't have the resources to set their adult children up for life after they are gone. We need help and we need it now. So many articles talk about children aging out of the system and having nothing to turn to, as if it is a new crisis. The crisis is not new. We have always been here. Watch the film *Wretches and Jabberers* to see one example of an intelligent and powerful Autistic man who personally lobbies with politicians, yet is homeless. There are Autistics of all ages – and I mean all, including people in their 70s and 80s – who have been living in crushing poverty for decades. It has been a silent crisis for too long. We need help now.

Q is for Quiet Hands Getting Loud

Quiet Hands. If you're Autistic, you are probably familiar with the phrase. It's the admonition to stop fidgeting, stop flapping, stop moving, stop what's called "stimming."

But "quiet hands" is not autism acceptance. It is part of the goal of so many autism therapies: to make an Autistic person "indistinguishable from their peers." People who try to accomplish this with Autistic people believe they're doing them a favor because they think that if we can just figure out how to look and act like everyone else around us who isn't Autistic, we will be "cured" and be able to have the same kind of "normal life" that other people have.

When I look around at myself and my fellow adults Autistics and hear their stories, it seems to me that this "indistinguishable from peers" goal is one that only a tiny fraction of Autistic people are even able to accomplish. Beyond the relative unattainability of "indistinguishable," the stress of trying to reach that goal can do long-term damage to a person's body and to their self-esteem.

The dirty truth about "quiet hands" and other attempts to train the autism out of us is that these sorts of therapies– teaching us to look others in the eye, stop fidgeting, stop rocking, stop doing anything that "looks too autistic"– are not really meant to help us. They are meant to make others feel more comfortable around us, to allow others to try to forget that we are Autistic.

Teaching us that we need to stop looking "too autistic" if we want to be treated with dignity and have a happy and productive life teaches us that who we are is wrong and ugly and unacceptable. And if we don't succeed in looking "normal enough," we have been taught to try to hide our autism, so our boss, co-workers, classmates, etc. don't understand why we are unusual. We are more likely to be bullied, shunned, and fired from our jobs if people don't realize that there is nothing "weird" or wrong about us; we're just Autistic. People are more likely to be willing to work alongside someone they know is Autistic than someone who is just "nebulously weird." I lost jobs for being considered too strange, creepy, etc. when it wasn't known that I am Autistic. Trying to teach Autistic people that the only route to success is to learn to fake being someone we aren't is setting most of us up for failure.

And the stress is long-lasting and can lead to health and functioning difficulties down the road. An excellent essay by Mel Baggs talks about the breaking point that people can face later in life after too many years of struggling through the stress and difficulty of "faking normal." In the section on burnout, Mel explains very clearly how years of "faking normal" can lead to a breakdown:

"Burnout, long-term shutdown, or whatever you want to call it, happens generally when you have been doing much more than you should be doing. Most people have a level to which they are capable of functioning without burnout, a level to which they are capable of functioning for emergency purposes only, and a level to which they simply cannot function. In autistic people in current societies, that first level is much narrower. Simply functioning at a minimally acceptable level to non-autistic people or for survival, can push us into the zone that in a non-autistic person would be reserved for emergencies. Prolonged functioning in emergency mode can result in loss of skills and burnout.

"With some diseases with long-term effects (and I am not suggesting that autism is a disease), it is the people who tried to ignore the long-term effects and "act normal" who often burn out, probably because they are drawing on emergency reserves to do so. There is a high chance that autistic people who attempt to ignore the fact that they are autistic and act like non-autistic people are subject to the same kind of burnout, or even autistic people who push themselves too hard in general without trying to look normal.

"The danger here may be obvious: It may be the people most capable of passing for normal, the most obvious 'success stories' in the eyes of non-autistic people (some of whom became so adept at passing that they were never considered autistic in the first place), who are the most likely to burn out the hardest and suddenly need to either act in very conspicuously autistic ways or die."[72]

If that sounds overly dramatic to you, it means that you still don't get it. You still don't really understand what it means to have a whole industry of therapy centered around making people do and say pointless and unnatural things so that they can look and sound like everyone else. Is there something about you that is different? Would you appreciate being told that you should spend your life dying your hair to hide the beautiful ginger shade you

72. From "Help! I Seem to be Getting More Autistic!" in the Autism Information Library. URL:
    http://archive.autistics.org/library/more-autistic.html

were born with? Have you ever recoiled in horror after learning that right handedness was so valued that left-handed children used to suffer having the bones in their hand broken so that they had no choice but to become right handed? Surely there's something about you that you have been pressured to hide and change? Dig into those memories to connect with what it means to be told that you were born wrong and need to spend the rest of your life pretending it wasn't so.

Teaching Quiet Hands isn't harmless. It teaches us that we are mistakes. It silences a big part of our voice. It seeks to shape our bodies in the image of some unrealistic ideal. And, for many of us, it reduces our ability to function.

I am a big fan of RPM, facilitated communication, typing or pointing at a letter board to communicate. I love to read the words of those who communicate with their hands. And one thing I have noticed many of those folks saying is that they can only communicate if they are allowed time to stim in between typing. Some flap their hands. Some twirl things like a special string. Some drop to the floor and roll back and forth. These kinds of motions– these very beautiful Autistic motions– help us to stay centered, to stay focused, to regulate huge emotions, to give needed input to nervous systems that do not function in the same way as those of most people around us.

When you force Autistic people to stop moving in the ways our bodies are made to move, you take away more than the appearances that are so uncomfortable for you to see. You very often clip our wings. You take away our ability to self-regulate. You might complain that we scream or cry too much but haven't noticed that we scream and cry less when we are allowed to live our truth on all levels. You may complain about how we complete a task – or how we are unable to complete a task– but you haven't noticed that we can do many things much better when we are able to do them in the ways that feel natural to us and when we are allowed to take those small breaks to do the things that make us feel better and more connected. We make sounds. We make faces. We move our loud hands. We move our bodies. We spin in circles, roll on the floor, sigh, stretch, wave our arms, fidget with jewelry. Whatever it is that we do, we don't do it to annoy you. In some cases we can stop doing those things but the cost is too high to justify asking us to stop.

Our quiet hands get loud and if you believe in autism acceptance you need to embrace our loud hands and understand why it is that our bodies need to sing.

R is for Relationships

This is such a huge topic, it would take an entire book to do it justice, but there are some very important highlights I need to hit when speaking of autism acceptance and relationships.

One of the questions parents of Autistic children ask most is "Will my child ever be able to have a relationship?" In darker moments, it's not even a question but rather a lament. "My poor, poor child! Autism has robbed them! They will never marry or have children!"

What these parents don't realize is that they're not quite asking the right questions. Too often, books about sex and relationships for parents of Autistics and for Autistic people ourselves make a basket of assumptions that can be very harmful to any developing young people but especially to young Autistic people, who so often need extra mentorship and guidance in life.

"Double Rainbow," a column on autism and sexuality, written by Caroline Narby and hosted by *Bitch Media,* has addressed these assumptions multiple times. Narby writes, "The aim of this blog is to explore and interrogate popular representations of autistic sexuality and gender performance from a queer, autistic perspective"[73] and goes on to say (speaking of a presentation in which it was strongly implied that autistic sexuality is only acceptable if it is mainstream with respect to gender and

73. URL: https://bitchmedia.org/post/double-rainbow-navigating-autism-gender-and-sexuality-feminism

sexuality), "There must have been young adults who are gay and/or genderqueer or trans*, or who are unsure of and are exploring their identities. The message they received was not that they are not alone and are worthy of love, but that they are undesirable. I know from first-hand experience that autistic youth are often already emotionally vulnerable. To be told that you are doubly broken, doubly unlovable and undesirable, because you are both autistic and queer, is devastating."

This is the big mistake I see so often in sex education targeted to Autistic people or our parents. The assumption is that everyone is heterosexual, everyone presents as the gender that matches the sex organs they were born with (and no one was born with ambiguous genitalia or chromosomes), and everyone wants to be in a sexual and romantic relationship. Sometimes, the erasure goes the other way and the book or speaker seems to believe that all Autistic people are completely asexual and aromantic. These kinds of stereotyped assumptions (that we're all cis-het, in other words, not trans and not queer, or all asexual) are very damaging to anyone who is taking those first steps into the world of adult relationships.

In my own case, I had the standard sex education that assumes everyone is cis-het (I was in middle and high school in the late 1970s and early 1980s) and I felt frightened and ashamed to try to talk to someone about the thoughts and feelings I had that were not part of that model. When I finally found an adult I could talk to, a local coordinator for PFLAG (Parents and Friends of Lesbians and Gays), she was wonderfully helpful, but made the assumption that I was a lesbian. Since no one told me about non-binary gender and sexuality, I accepted what she wrote to me (I was too shy to call for advice so I had written a letter to her) and I worked hard to fit in with my presumed lesbian identity, unaware that there were other ways of being a sexual person.

As it turns out, I am panromantic and grey ace. If you don't know what those words mean, first think of bisexual– a concept you're probably at least somewhat familiar with– and now think about what bisexuality looks like when there are more than two genders to choose from. Since I now understand that gender is not strictly a binary[74] I can't really call myself bisexual because that

74. There are cis-females, cis-males, trans-women, trans-men, intersex folks, genderqueer folks, third gender folks, and all kinds of other flavors I don't have time or space to go into here....

word implies that there are only two choices and I have had loving relationships with people of many different genders. Bear in mind, though, that, some people who are panromantic or pansexual have chosen to reclaim the words bisexual and biromantic for various reasons and re-shape it into a non-binary meaning, so don't assume that someone who identifies as bi* is supporting the notion of a strict gender binary by calling themselves bisexual or biromantic.

Grey ace means that I fall somewhere on the asexual spectrum. This has been a complicated identity for me to communicate to others, because I'm not purely asexual, that is completely uninterested in sex. But when I say "the stars must align before I become sexual," rest assured that what I'm describing is not just that I need to get to know someone well before I get physically involved with them. My libido is not even linked to bodies and genitals but to events that the vast majority of people would not consider sexual events.

If you wonder why I'm giving so much detail about my own sexuality, it's because I don't want my fellow adult Autistics with "quirky" orientations to feel so alone and I want parents of Autistic children to get used to hearing about and trying to understand non-mainstream sexual, romantic, and gender identities because there's a high chance you will be hearing similar things one day from your child and their friends.

Because I am often quite literal-minded and because I accepted that the adults around me knew the truth and could teach it to me, my struggle to be "a good lesbian" was just as difficult and shame-inducing as my struggle to be "a good straight girl." Neither one was working for me, and I didn't understand why for a long time. Of course this sort of identity struggle can happen to anyone, Autistic or not. But, for many reasons, we are extra-vulnerable to these sorts of difficulties in understanding our identity. We need an atmosphere of openness when we are making those first steps of self-discovery.

Now . . . I realize that I'm talking about things that are complex and sometimes subtle. It can be intimidating to try to figure out how to introduce all this complexity when you're terrified just to talk about sex at all with your Autistic child. Or maybe you are nervous because right now you're working on helping your child learn that touching their genitals is something they can't do in the grocery store. Or at church. Take a breath and remember the joke: "How do you eat an elephant?"

"One bite at a time." Deal with whatever you and your child are dealing with right at this moment. The sexuality issues I'm discussing here might seem lightyears away from what our child is currently going through, but don't dismiss the idea that your child has a sexual identity just because you can't see evidence of it at the moment. And try to work on opening up your language and your mind to the thought that your child might be gay. Or heterosexual. Or pansexual. Or asexual. Or transgender. Or . . .

Let your child set the cues as far as gendered clothing. I see a lot of sex advice for Autistic young women that tries to convince us to put on make up or shave our legs or wear a dress instead of jeans and a sweatshirt. Some of us like to do those things. Some of us LOVE to do those things. And some of the Autistics who love to shave their legs and wear a dress and make up were born into a body with a penis. Focus on good grooming and let your child teach you what their sense of fashion is. Don't try to force an Autistic young person to dress a particular way. We often learn– either through difficult therapies or just through living a life where too often we are told how wrong we are– to be extra-compliant, and that can extend to trying to please others by dressing, speaking, and behaving in a way that feels completely unnatural to us. So often, we grow up feeling we have no choice but to comply and conform. Be aware of this and try not to unconsciously (or consciously!) force your child into a sex and gender mold that is not a good fit for them.

And all that "my child will never get married and have children" angst? I can understand why that upsets you, but you need to work on privately getting past that. Talk to your partner, if you have any, about those fears. Talk to a therapist or a close friend. Don't write it in any place, public or private, that your child is likely to see some day, and don't think that just because your child doesn't speak or interact with others right now that they will never read and understand things. You can't guess your child's life trajectory and you might come to learn that everything you said in front of them, thinking they didn't understand, went straight into their emotions and their memory. What if your child grows up to be an asexual adult? Or an adult who consciously chooses not to have children? How will your child feel about your misery over the thought that they will never marry or have children if it turns out that they really don't want to marry or have children? Do you think your child will feel accepted for who they truly are?

Everyone raising children needs to learn about different forms of sexual expression (or non-expression by choice).   Did you know that someone can be asexual but not aromantic? Some people who are asexual still want a loving and emotionally bonded relationship. Some do not. Some people fall in love with more than one person at the same time and choose to have relationships that are honest and open and not monogamous. It is important for every parent to learn about sex, gender, relationships, and love so that they are prepared to support their beloved child no matter what road of life that child grows up to travel. If you believe in autism acceptance, and you agree with the neurodiversity movement, you need to accept sexuality and gender diversity. Autistic people end up non-cis and/or non-het at the same rate as the general population . . . Or possibly even more often.[75] Just as autism is a core piece of who we are, sexuality and gender are deep and pervasive. To accept one and not the other is just as damaging as accepting neither.

S is for Stop Saying Savant Syndrome and Splinter Skills

When you see an Autistic person who is very talented at something, are you tempted to call them a savant? Don't. I realize you mean to compliment them, but the word is loaded and ableist. You may already realize that talking about splinter skills is ableist, or, if you aren't deeply involved in the medical aspects of autism, you might not be familiar with the term.   I'm going to

---

75. URL: http://online.liebertpub.com/doi/10.1089/trgh.2015.0007

unpack them both, showing why these are words you should never use to describe people's abilities. Let's start with "savant."

Joseph Straus, a professor at CUNY, examines the history of the term "savant" in "Idiots Savants, Retarded Savants, Talented Aments, Mono-Savants, Autistic Savants, Just Plain Savants, People with Savant Syndrome, and Autistic People Who Are Good at Things: A View from Disability Studies," a paper published in *Disability Studies Quarterly*. As Straus points out, the original term was "idiot savant" and it was generally applied to people who were intellectually disabled, but who could perform in one area brilliantly. Sometimes that area was math, sometimes music, sometimes art. The point of the label was to highlight the juxtaposition of "extreme incompetence" and "extreme competence." Not only were the term and the ideas behind it offensive and ableist, it was a way of stating what society finds valuable or worthless about a person. The brilliant musicianship, for example, was valuable because people liked to hear the music and would pay money to listen. The "idiot" nature of the rest of the person's life was considered worthless.

Straus tells us that the idea of the "autistic savant" is fairly new and can largely be attributed to the popularity of the Dustin Hoffman and Tom Cruise film *Rain Man*, in which Hoffman plays Raymond Babbitt, an Autistic adult. Hoffman's character was modeled after two people: Kim Peek, a non-autistic "savant"; and William Sackter, a non-autistic man with a learning disability who was institutionalized (the state said he would be a "burden on society" otherwise) in the Faribault State School for the Feeble-Minded and Epileptic after his father died of Spanish Flu. Sackter, who was portrayed by actor Mickey Rooney in a film about his life called *Bill*, was tested after 44 years of institutionalization and found to have an I.Q. in the normal range. He had been a victim of the over-institutionalization of "problem people" that was rampant in the 1920s.

Bear in mind, the largest outrage is not that Sackter was not actually "feeble-minded." The largest outrage is that *anyone* was locked away in such a state school. People who complain of over-diagnosis of children today are forgetting that so many of today's mainstreamed children with IEPs and classroom aides would have been invisible behind the walls of an institution in the past. Chances are, Sackter had something like dyslexia or ADHD. Do not mourn alleged overdiagnosis; rejoice at de-institutionalization.

Hoffman's portrayal of autism, built upon the presentations of two non-autistic people, set the tone of public discourse for decades. Public understanding of what autism looks like has, until recently, largely been centered around Hoffman's portrayal. The "Rain Man" concept of adult autism still lingers, though it has largely been replaced with a blend of Temple Grandin and the fictional character Sheldon Cooper from television's *Big Bang Theory*. Raymond Babbitt was institutionalized, exhibited repetitive speech, needed supervision and assistance, and could count large numbers of things nearly instantly. In one scene, a server in a restaurant drops a box of toothpicks on the floor and Raymond instantly counts them. At first, his count is believed to be in error but when the server reveals that 4 toothpicks were left in the box, everyone is amazed. Raymond also memorized the phone book, halfway through the Gs, after his brother, Charlie, gave it to him in frustration to shut Raymond up, telling him "here, read this!" (A suggestion Raymond accepts with placid literalness.)

Charlie notices Raymond's impressive memory and counting skills and teaches him to illegally count cards before taking him to Vegas to win lots of money. Charlie doesn't really like Raymond. He is frustrated with Raymond's echolalia and with his need for structure in little things like what brand of underwear he wears or whether the maple syrup is on the table before or after the pancakes, but Charlie does value Raymond's ability to count and remember because it can be monetized.

This is where the notion of an "autistic savant" is dehumanizing. Have you ever heard someone called a savant because they collect bus transfers (as I used to do in my early teen years) and know every detail about the different transfers and the system for using them? Or what about someone who has memorized every detail of every episode of Dr. Who, all the way back to 1963? No, I'm pretty sure you've never heard those folks called savants, and there's a reason. "Savant" is code for "can do something society finds useful." That's why people called savants do things like make music or art or count fast, memorize well, calculate very large numbers accurately and so on.

To say that someone is a savant is to say several things:

- that they are incompetent in every area of their life except one
- that they have value that is contingent on their heightened skill in that one area
- that others who are judged incompetent and do not have a "savant" skill are not valuable
- that this person is a "freak," a social outsider, an Other

When someone can do a thing that you find amazing, do not discount their competence in other areas of life. They may need guidance or assistance from friends and other helpers. That does not mean that they are incompetent. If you value their ability to multiply five digit numbers in their head and devalue the rest of their life because they are unable to work or because they need accommodations or assistance, you are setting yourself up to miss the very real humanity and joy of knowing that person. You are commodifying their mathematical abilities and dismissing their personhood. You are reducing them to a biological adding machine.

People have inherent value and should not be valued solely on whether they are "useful" or not. Nazi Germany called disabled people "Nutlos Esser" (useless eaters) and said they lived a "ballast existence," holding the rest of the country back with their needs for extra care and their lack of useful productivity. As a result, disabled people were the first to die. The Aktion T4 program was a trial run for the larger exterminations of Jews, Romany, Homosexuals, Polish, etc. This is what happens to disabled people who are valued only for what they can produce.[76]

You may be tempted to invoke Godwin's Law and say I am going too far in speaking of Nazi death camps when I talk about why the term "savant" is dangerous. Don't forget that the Nazis did not invent eugenics– it was an American export. Don't forget that disabled women and Women of Color were being involuntarily sterilized in the United States as recently as the 1970s. Don't forget that Kissinger's *National Security Study Memorandum 200*, written in 1974, described "overpopulation" in less

---

76. Wikipedia entry: https://en.wikipedia.org/wiki/Action_T4

developed countries as a security threat, saying that U.S. policy should include, "pay[ing] women in the LDCs to have abortions as a method of family planning or to pay persons to perform abortions or to solicit persons to undergo abortions."[77] In other words, he suggested a "soft" genocide of poor, non-white people. Poor women all over the world, including in the United States, are offered money to be sterilized. I was offered $300 to be sterilized in 1991, solely because I was on food stamps and unable to keep a job. I turned the offer down.

This is a world where the poor are blamed and punished for their poverty. Politicians campaign on a platform of taking food stamps away from "those who refuse to work" despite the fact that, according to the Frequently Asked Questions on the U.S. government's SNAP website, at least 40% of food stamp households do have at least one working member and 75% of food stamp households have children. Sixteen percent of food stamp households include a disabled person and 9% include seniors.[78]

If I haven't managed to clarify why it is dangerous to predicate people's value on their usefulness, I don't know what else to say.

Promoting the idea of the autistic savant harms Autistic people. I know someone who endured a person throwing toothpicks at their feet and asking them how many there were. Seriously. The idea that some Autistics are "savants" impairs many people's ability to see us as human beings and treat us accordingly. Yes many of us are really, really good at some things. That is not because Autistics are savants but rather because the Autistic mind latches on to things it loves and savors them thoroughly. Some Autistics love animals. Some love Thomas the Tank Engine. Some love industrial deep fryers. Some love the work of Neil Gaiman. Some love languages. Some love flags. It's okay. It's not "savant syndrome." It's people who are hard-wired to really get into the things they love. Focusing on the things we love gives us immense joy. If you have never gotten really deeply into something, so far that you were eating, breathing, and dreaming about it, you will not understand this joy. You don't have to be Autistic to experience it, but it helps.

77. URL: http://pdf.usaid.gov/pdf_docs/PCAAB500.pdf
78. URL: http://www.snaptohealth.org/snap/snap-frequently-asked-questions/

"It's that the experience is so rich. It's textured, vibrant, and layered. It exudes joy. It is a hug machine for my brain. It makes my heart pump faster and my mouth twitch back into a smile every few minutes. I feel like I'm sparkling. Every inch of me is totally engaged in and powered up by the obsession. Things are clear.

"It is beautiful. It is perfect."

– Julia Bascom[79]

This is not a separate competence in a desert of incompetence. This is an Autistic way of being. It is whole and to call it "savant syndrome" is to cut us into little pieces so you can say that you approve of this piece but that piece has just got to go.

That is exactly what the phrase "splinter skills" does. It cuts us into little pieces, into splinters. It says "this part of you is good but those parts of you are bad." It splinters us into fragments of worth and worthlessness. It declares us incomplete people, less than fully human, splintered.

How would you like it if your ability to bake amazing brownies were called a splinter skill– you are judged incompetent, except when it comes to brownies. You can solve partial differential equations? Great splinter skill. Too bad you don't know how to change the oil in your car or you would be a real person.

Ariane, the mother of Emma, a fabulously Autistic young woman, writes, "If we did the same thing to those who are born without Autism, if we talked about our non-Autistic neurology as a deficit and identified all the ways in which it would cause us problems and difficulty, would we not despair when our non-autistic child was born as well? Take your own life as an example and imagine that when you were born you were seen as a great disappointment. Think about how each time you did something well it was dismissed as a 'splinter skill' and was seen as yet another example of all that

---

79. URL: https://juststimming.wordpress.com/2011/04/05/the-obsessive-joy-of-autism/

was 'wrong' with you."[80]

Mayer Shevin, who just passed away in 2014, wrote an iconic poem, "The Language of Us/Them." In it, he writes, "We have talents / They have splinter skills,"[81] highlighting how differently ability is viewed among the Autistic compared to the general population.

And if you were wondering how you should refer to Autistic people with talent, now that you know that "savant" and "splinter" are unacceptable words, there it is. We have talents. We have abilities. We have passions. Speak of our skills as skills, not as freakish anomalies. Discuss what we can do the way you would discuss what any other human being can do. Whether it is Roadrunner cartoons or astrophysics, call it a talent, a skill, an aptitude. And celebrate it, whether it is a marketable skill or not. Because these are the things that bring the most joy into our lives.

To discover what an Autistic loves, listen to what we know.

To value an Autistic person, value who we are, not who we could be or what we could make of ourselves.

It really is that simple. Be with us as we are. Know us without agenda and value us without a price tag.

This is the heart of autism acceptance. If you value us completely, for every part of us– not just the splinters– you will surely come to love us.

T is for Toe-walking, Trauma, and Truth-telling

Toe-walking is a very common trait among those with developmental disabilities, particularly Autistics. While walking around on tip-toes all or most of the time can also indicate things like cerebral palsy or congenitally

---

80. URL: https://emmashopebook.com/2013/03/20/splinter-skills-and-other-words-we-use/
81. URL:http://nursefriendly.com/nursing/inspiration/the.language.of.us.them.mayer.shevin.htm

tight Achilles tendons, it's most often associated with autism. The fact is, all children walk on their tip toes sometimes. Most children stop doing it much or at all somewhere between the ages of 2 and 5. Autistic children tend to keep toe-walking a lot. Plenty of adults still toe-walk and I used to be one of them, but I had to train myself to stop doing it over the course of the last ten years because I have a connective tissue disorder called Ehlers-Danlos Syndrome (EDS), and I am trying to cope with the physical damage caused by 40 years of toe-walking in a body with seriously flawed tendons.

Toe walking has always seemed natural to me. I remember being reprimanded often in my pre-teen years whenever I was seen toe-walking. I honestly tried to stop doing it, but as soon as my attention wandered away from my feet, I'd be right back up on my toes again. I remember my mother taking me to a doctor to discuss the options. He talked about surgery or putting casts on my feet. My mother felt those options were too extreme (and I tend to agree with her), so she tried to just help train me not to do it anymore– a task that sounds easier than it actually was, because toe-walking was comfortable for me, making it a deeply persistent trait.

I have learned that toe-walking up to middle-age can be dangerous. I know other adult Autistics who still toe-walk and have no physical difficulties as a result, but combined with EDS, toe-walking has been very damaging to me. My tendons have shortened and I get injured more easily. In fact, I have been nursing a foot injury for nearly a year now. I sleep with foot braces that hold my feet in a position that helps stretch my Achilles tendons. I limp a lot. I am in pain nearly constantly. It is because decades of toe-walking with a connective tissue condition[82] will re-shape your feet in many detrimental ways. Because of those changes and the injuries I've sustained, I'm sometimes forced to take a few steps on tip-toe as I "warm up" and stretch out the tendons for flat-footed walking or else I couldn't walk at all.

So here's the first connection: toe-walking can cause lasting trauma, but in addition to the physical trauma I have from decades of toe-walking, I also live

---

82. And did I mention that EDS appears to be more common among those on the autism spectrum than in the general population?

with the psychological trauma of being repeatedly corrected for toe-walking. It's a tricky thing. All the times I was told to stop toe-walking made an impression on me and kind of melted in with all the other times I was corrected for all the other things that were either beyond my control or so deeply ingrained that I often felt that I was spending every ounce of my focus on remembering not to do the countless things I was always being told not to do. I was juggling too many "thou shalt nots" at once, and it was overwhelming to me.

I don't have an easy answer to how to help steer an Autistic person without making them feel traumatized by feeling like they are always being told that they are doing everything wrong, but here's a good place to start: don't try to "fix" everything. Hand-flapping? Not a problem. Work on educating the rest of the world that hand-flapping is a harmless motion that some people engage in for various reasons. Don't try to normalize the person; normalize hand-flapping. My best friend hand-flaps sometimes in loving imitation of me when I'm excited. I find it charming. He is not put off by the ways I move and it is a dear way for him to show how "normal" he finds it.

This is one of the problems with therapies that seek to make us "indistinguishable from our peers." If you try to stop us from doing anything that looks Autistic, you will be constantly picking at us to stop almost everything we do and we will feel overwhelmed and traumatized. So pick your battles. Hand-flapping is fine. Focus on things like not hitting siblings, keeping body waste inside diapers or toilets, not biting others, not banging one's head against hard things . . . and for those of us at risk of damage from it, toe-walking. Don't worry about it at a pre-school age. Every pre-schooler toe-walks some amount, often a lot. But gradually work on flat-footed walking. If your child is receptive to verbal reasoning, explain to them what can happen if they spend too much time on tip-toes. It's not too different from what happens to women who wear very high heels a lot (although it can be more damaging. Imagine if women started wearing high heels every single moment of every single day at, oh, age two or so, when their feet are still forming and growing), so it shouldn't be too hard to find some information and other first-hand accounts of the long-term damage toe-walking over the course of many years can cause.

Toe-walking is a body-truth and trauma can be caused both by decades of toe-walking and by trying to correct toe-walking too vehemently (especially while trying to "correct" everything else, most of which does not need correcting).

Trauma is a big deal for autism acceptance. I believe that many of us Autistics are more easily traumatized by some things than other people are. I also think that many of us Autistics have had to endure things that are more traumatizing than a childhood (or adulthood) ought to be, and I think trauma often puts us at odds with ourselves when it comes to truth-telling.

There is a myth that Autistics are incapable of lying. It's wrong. We can lie. Many of us aren't very good at it. I hate lying for several reasons, but one of the biggest reasons I hate it is because I'm just so darned bad at it. It's stressful to try to keep up with a lie. It's stressful to get caught out when lying. It's stressful to feel bad because I'd rather not be lying. Chavisory commented on my blog that one reason she loves the story of Donald Triplett, the first person diagnosed with autism, telling others how many bricks were in the façade of a building is because he admitted later in an *Atlantic Monthly* article that he had lied and made up the number. She loves how that busts the stereotype of Autistics as being incapable of lying. Triplett knew that the people asking wouldn't check to see if he was right and because they were so interested in seeing if he knew (and he was so eager to win their admiration) he lied and made up a number. And got away with it. Autistics can lie. We are more likely to tell the truth, even if it's an uncomfortable or angering truth, but we *can* lie.

Trauma can rob us of the choice to tell the truth. For example, if we are traumatized enough about a particular aspect of our behavior, we may resort to lying in order to avoid getting reprimanded yet again. For many of us, too, lying is traumatizing in itself, and so trauma can re-traumatize again and again by forcing us to lie. Truth-telling and trauma are linked. If you always get shouted at or even physically punished for doing something that you can't help doing, you start to get sneaky and learn ways to hide it or lie about it. Pretty soon, you start feeling like your whole life is a lie and all you are doing is trying to maneuver around the trauma spots without getting caught.

This is not just Autistics. Anyone forced to live a lie can come to feel traumatized by the constant requirement of pretense. It doesn't matter if it's a gay teen trying to hide their identity from judgmental parents who might kick them out of the house, or a Black person who has to be constantly aware of how they move, look, speak, walk, and so on in order to avoid being accused of shoplifting or worse, or an Autistic struggling to not flap their hands, pretend to maintain eye contact (but not too much eye contact!), and speak in ways that other people expect them to. Living a lie is stressful and traumatizing.

Encourage the Autistic people in your life to be truth-tellers– not by threatening punishment if they lie, but rather by setting up an environment where it is okay to be who they really are and where even dangerous or destructive actions are met first with an attempt to understand why the person needs those actions, then by helping to find alternatives and lovingly mentoring the Autistic to be the best, safest, healthiest, most free, and truest Autistic they can be.   Recognize how easy it is to traumatize someone by outlawing everything that is natural to them, and don't compound trauma by pushing them so hard to be someone they aren't and forcing them to lie about things – especially things that are so much a part of who they naturally are.

Autism acceptance means helping, mentoring, guiding, but never trying to re-shape an Autistic person for no good reason beyond the comfort of others. If you accept Autistic people, you will accept that we often move differently, communicate differently, and think differently. Autism acceptance does not mean just letting us "go wild." We need mentoring just like anyone else. Autism acceptance means working to understand why we do things and carefully discerning before you try to change our behavior: Do you want to change it to help us be healthier and happier? Or do you want to change it because you think other people will not accept us the way we are?

If you think people will not accept us because we look, think, and communicate differently, do not try to make us into people we aren't. If you think we will not be accepted, you must work to change the world into one that can accept people regardless of neurology, color of skin, religion, or any other of the myriad things that contribute to the glorious diversity of human beings.

Do not traumatize us in the name of helping us fit in.

Do not try to make us smaller; work to make the world's heart bigger.

U is for Unity

"The point in history at which we stand is full of promise and danger. The world will either move toward unity and widely shared prosperity – or it will move apart." – Franklin D. Roosevelt[83]

Which direction have we moved since Roosevelt's warning?

I look around me and see a world that is struggling to move toward unity, but that still has a long way to go toward that goal. Compared with that point in history at which Roosevelt was speaking, we have made much progress in unity among people who are racially diverse, who adhere to diverse religions or no religion, who have different genders. We have passed the Americans with Disabilities Act (ADA) and work daily to enforce it. We have taken steps to address class and income inequality. Yet we see racial conflict daily and the United States is still a place where white people benefit, mostly unconsciously, from institutionalized racism. We still see battles between adherents of different religions, mistrust and discrimination against people based on religion– particularly discrimination directed toward Muslim Americans, mistrust and fear directed toward atheists,[84] employment glass ceilings for women and those of minority genders, ableism and abuse of disabled people both in institutions and homes, sheltered

83. URL: http://www.ibiblio.org/pha/policy/1945/450212a.html
84. An academic study of public opinion found that more people would trust a known rapist than would trust a known atheist. URL: http://psycnet.apa.org/psycinfo/2011-25187-001/

workshops where disabled people are paid pennies for their work, and an income gap that is wider than it has been at any time since the Great Depression.

Autism acceptance demands joining the struggle toward unity. When I call for unity, I'm not saying that everyone should be the same as everyone else. I am talking about the kind of unity composer Felix Mendelssohn spoke of when he said, "the essence of beauty is unity in variety," or the unity of George Herbert Mead's declaration that "society is unity in diversity." I am calling for an understanding of our interconnectedness coupled with a respect for human diversity in all spheres of our being, including, of course, neurodiversity. Autism Speaks recently said that the neurodiversity movement in general and Steve Silberman's book *Neurotribes* specifically were damaging efforts toward unity in the autism community, largely because we are breaking down the authority of ABA and demanding that Autistic people be treated with dignity and humanity. To this claim of our destruction of the unity of oppression Autistics have faced for generations, I respond with the words of Nick Walker:[85] "What the vulture calls unity, the giraffe calls getting eaten."

So what is the unity that I am talking about? For starters, we need to reach out beyond our own borders. In my experience, Autistic people and our allies are too often isolated from the larger disability community. Ari Ne'eman, the co-founder of the Autistic Self-Advocacy Network (ASAN) and the first Autistic person to serve on the National Council on Disability, spoke of this separation in a roundtable discussion in 2012, saying:

"I think we have a tremendous amount to learn from the larger disability world, and I fear this is something that autism does not do a very good job of. No one who had absorbed the lessons of Willowbrook and Pennhurst would think it was a good idea to build special 'Gated Communities' to house autistic adults and others with intellectual and developmental disabilities. No one who knows the history of the Jerry Lewis telethon and the objections made by people with muscular

85. Nick blogs at *Neurocosmopolitanism*. URL: http://neurocosmopolitanism.com/

dystrophy to being portrayed as pitiful, 'half-people' by its star would ever conceive of something like the 'I Am Autism' video. No one who knew the names Ed Roberts, Judy Heumann or Justin Dart and the history of all they accomplished for people with disabilities would ever doubt the meaning and importance of self-advocacy by and for us, instead of on our behalf. Yet, these are not things we think about or have even heard of in the autism world."[86]

Things are slowly changing since Ne'eman made these observations, but still so much of the world of autism is isolated. Mainly, it is Autistic academics and activists who are venturing beyond our borders, but the larger Autistic/autism community is opening to wider unity all the time. We are forging close alliance with others with developmental disabilities, particularly people with Down Syndrome and Cerebral Palsy, but our connections don't stop there. The larger disability community has battled an internal schism for years and the time is ripe for Autistic activists to join the fight against internal ableism. For so many years, many of those with mobility disabilities and other physical disabilities have said things like, "my body is impaired but my mind is strong and good." This is a very understandable thing to say, but it created a climate unfriendly to those with neurological and psychiatric disabilities. The larger disability community is strongly challenging those attitudes now, though, and as a result there is increased unity among people of diverse disabilities, increased solidarity, and an increased ability for all of us to work together for the rights of all of us.

It is time for Autistics and our friends, families, and allies to join the larger fight. It is time for us to turn our attention outward and work to help others as we allow them to help us. We are all connected through the shared experience of disability. Our disabilities are different– just as each Autistic person has their own individual experience of autism– but the stigma and social barriers we face are strikingly similar. Autistic people and the rest of the disability community have much to offer each other. I think many Autistic people and their supporters shy away from working within the larger

---

86. URL: http://www.huffingtonpost.com/seth-mnookin/autism-roundtable-crossdi_b_1232699.html

disability community because of fear of that word, "disabled." That fear points to an internal division within the Autistic/autism community that needs to be mended as well.

Within the Autistic community, there is a schism not terribly different from the brain/body schism the larger disability community is working to heal. Within our community, there are those who insist on only portraying autism's strengths, who fear words like "disability," who cling to the label "Asperger's" which is no longer a diagnostic category, at least not here in the U.S., and is in the process of fading into the past as a piece of medical and autistic history, not unlike other terms such as "dementia praecox," "manic-depression," or "sexual inversion." Now that all forms of autism have been united under a single label, the main purpose (other than historical) of the word "Asperger's" is to draw an "us vs. them" distinction within the neurotribe of autism. It is a "dog whistle" that speaks a code of "functioning labels" and supremacy. It is a way to say, "don't mistake us for *those* people who wear adult diapers and a head-restraining device." It is a way to maintain division within the community.

And division will not move us closer to unity.

And autism acceptance demands unity.

Autistic people who say "different, not disabled" need to stop and think about the message they are putting forth. Because of their fear of being considered less-than, because of their fear of taking on the stigma fellow Autistics live with every day, because they are hovering at the fringes of activism and advocacy, trying to "pass" as non-autistic and focus only on Autistic strengths while often diminishing or dismissing Autistic needs, they are actively working to increase division in the community. Those who don't have the privilege of passing, even for a short time, are left out of their description of Autism. In insisting that autism is not a disability, they drain the compassion of those who would otherwise want to assist and accommodate us. In insisting that autism is not a disability, they help make the overall movement of autistic advocacy and self-advocacy look like a game or a collection of lies– anyone who knows or is an Autistic person who cannot pass and requires accommodation can see right through that game and can see the harm it does to the larger Autistic community.

Autism is a difference AND a disability. Disability does not mean "incapable of anything." It does not mean "less than." It simply means having some traits that contribute to some limits– both inherently (such as not being able to speak or not being able to recognize faces) and socially (such as being passed over for jobs because of a cultural lack of belief in the competence of a particular category of people). When Autistic people face challenges, such as difficulty in face-to-face conversations, and social limitations, such as only 15% of people diagnosed Autistic having full-time jobs at the level of which they are capable of working, autism is undeniably a disability. The bulk of the disability of autism is external, placed upon us by the judgments of others, but socially-imposed disability is disability nonetheless. Arguing against the disability of autism is arguing against a united voice that advocates for the needs of all of us. Arguing against autism as a disability is arguing against our unity.

It is not just unity within our own group and unity with the larger disability community that we are called to support. We need to seek unity with all marginalized people, all people who face oppression. We need to seek unity with People of Color, with people of all genders, especially transgender, non-gender, intersex, and other minority-gender people. We need to seek unity with everyone who suffers discrimination for who they are. It is in this way that we fight against a society that holds up a monolithic notion of "normal" and "perfect" that is oppressive to everyone, but especially to those who fall outside society's "circle of virtue."

It is only through seeking unity that we can protect other vulnerable and marginalized people and, in fairness, hope for them to protect us. Many people in our own neurotribe are multiply marginalized, so when we support the rights and needs of impoverished people, People of Color, people of diverse gender expressions and so forth, we are supporting and protecting our own Autistic siblings as well as reaching out to the larger community and working toward a realization of that interconnectedness all humans share. Seeking unity with all people helps build that just and prosperous society Roosevelt dreamed of. Seeking unity makes us all part of the solution, not part of the problem.

It is worth paraphrasing Martin Niemöller's famous poem about Word War II Germany and persecution under the Nazi regime:[87]

First they oppressed the People of Color
and I did not speak out
because I was white.
Then they oppressed the Transgender People
and I did not speak out
because I identify with the sex I was assigned at birth.
Then they oppressed the Psychiatrically Disabled
and I did not speak out
because I had not been diagnosed with a mental illness.
Then they oppressed those Autistics Who Needed Round the Clock Care
and I did not speak out
because I was able to live independently.
Then they came for me
and there was no one left
to speak out for me.

This is our lesson, this is our mission, this is our clarion call: unity.

V is for Vulnerable to Violence and Victimization

It is ironic that so many people fear us when Autistic people are much more likely to be subject to violence and abuse than to perpetrate it against

87. Source URL at the People's History of the Holocaust & Genocide website:
    http://remember.org/witness/links-let-niem

others. I'm not saying that we are incapable of being harmful or abusive. Yes, there have been abusive Autistic people and Autistic people who have a difficult time controlling anger.   But violence is less common among us and we are so vulnerable and, in some cases, so naïve that we can be easy targets for predators and abusers. In fact, I've discovered that there are some predators who single us out intentionally, because we are Autistic and thus easier to manipulate, more likely to have a weak personal support system to protect us, and more likely to have gone through compliance training that teaches us to accept abuse as a normal part of life.

Now, I know I've already talked about bullying in an earlier chapter, but when I talk about violence and victimization, I'm talking about something even more sinister. There are predators out there who seek out disabled children and adults specifically. They've been called "disability trolls"– people who have sexual fetishes for disabilities and make fake online profiles to try to get close to people in wheelchairs, amputees, and other physically disabled people.[88] What makes things less clear when it comes to Autism is that there are some predators who specifically seek out Autistic people and others who just seem to have a radar for vulnerability. A large percentage of the people they prey on are Autistic, but maybe more as a coincidence, due to Autistic people having a tendency toward more vulnerability than the general population.

A 1991 study[89] found that not only are people with disabilities sexually abused more often than the general population, but that the abuse tends to be repeated again and again, chronically. The researchers found that 49% of people with intellectual disability will experience sexual abuse or assault 10 or more times in their lives. Another study published in 2000[90] found that people who are multiply disabled are at greater risk of sexual assault and

88. "Creepy Is As Creepy Does: The Secret World of Disability Trolls" by Eric P. Kondo Not-Me.org, 2013. This is a booklet about disability fetishists or "disability trolls", aimed at helping disabled people steer clear of users and abusers. URL: http://www.not-me.org/creepyisascreepydoes.pdf
89. "Patterns of Sexual Abuse and Assault" by Sobsey and Doe. *Sexuality and Disability*, Volume 9, Issue 3, September 1991, pp 243-59.
90. "Maltreatment and Disabilities: A Population-based Epidemiological Study" by Sullivan and Knutson. *Child Abuse and Neglect*, Volume 24, Issue 10, October 2000, pp. 1257-73.

abuse. The disabled people most likely to be abused were those with intellectual disabilities, communication disabilities, and behavioral disabilities– all of which are disabilities often found alongside autism. In short, disabled people are more than three times more likely to be assaulted and abused than the general population and Autistic people, particularly Autistic women, are among the most assaulted and abused of all disabled people. The 1991 study found 83% of women with developmental disabilities had been sexually assaulted at least once in their lives.

The victimization is not just sexual. A study of disabled people using a third-party payment system[91] (disability benefits being sent to someone other than the disabled person themselves, typically a caregiver or financial manager) found that 20% of the third-party recipients were victims of crimes ranging from larceny to murder and "slave trading," a practice where disabled people are bought and sold from payee to payee, getting little or no actual care and being valued only for their benefit check. Additionally, the victimization of disabled people is greatly downplayed. It is often reported in the system and in the media as "abuse and neglect," as opposed to naming the actual crimes that occurred, such as rape, assault, or murder. Crimes against disabled people often go unreported altogether due to being committed by people upon whom the disabled person depends for survival. As bad as the situation appears– and the appearance is quite bad enough– the reality is much, much worse.

Those who have read my previous book, *No You Don't*, or the title essay from the collection, know that I have had a long history of victimization spanning decades. At this point in my life, I have learned most of the ways predators enlist victims and am, thankfully, able to avoid the kinds of abuse and exploitation that marred my childhood, teens, twenties, thirties, and parts of my forties. But I am still vulnerable, and I had a run-in with a predator just a few years ago.   I am skeptical, a quick learner, a reflective thinker, and have excellent pattern recognition, but I have

---

91. "Crime Victims with Developmental Disabilities: A Review Essay" by Joan R. Petersilia. *Criminal Justice and Behavior*, Volume 28, Number 6, December 2001, pp. 655-94.

difficulty when things stray too far from what I've experienced and categorized before. It has made it harder for me to learn how to avoid being victimized because if the approach happens in a different way or a different place, or even something simple is changed like the gender or age of the predator, I can fall for the same thing all over again, feeling foolish afterward when I make the connection and realize that I missed seeing a pattern that looks very clear in retrospect.

There are many other factors leading to re-victimization as well. A few of them include: not being able to figure out how to break out of a repeated "script," being too afraid of offending or making someone angry, lacking strong boundaries (often due to the abuses of compliance-based "therapies," including ABA), being lonely and having too little social experience to raise skepticism about offers of instant friendship from strangers.

My predator from a few years ago was hard for me to spot in part because I have grown accustomed to predators who want sexual attention from me or who want my money (meager though it is). This predator was looking for something else. I'm not entirely sure what they were seeking, but it involved receiving attention, validation, and admiration, as well as gaining control over others. When they made their first overture to me– offering to mail me a present– they seemed safe and trustworthy because we had 62 mutual friends on Facebook. The huge overlap of our friends' lists made them seem legitimate and a trusted member of the autism/Autistic community. I had never noticed the person before so I don't know how long they had been in my community.

I now will not accept a friend request from someone unless I have at least talked to them a little, and I periodically "purge" my friends list of the people who "friended and forgot." They rapidly become an unknown stranger on my friend list if they don't interact with me. Even those precautions have not prevented my Facebook account from becoming overwhelming and an unwelcoming place for me to be. I am still trying to figure out what my personal Facebook policy should be. It hasn't worked out very well for me the way I have been doing it. I did find a plug-in that turns off the newsfeed and just that one change has vastly improved my Facebook experience, though it's still a very difficult medium of interaction for me. Online socializing turns out to be nearly as overwhelming and anxiety-inducing for me as face-to-face socialization.

It took me a while to figure out what I had gotten into with this particular predator on Facebook. They seemed so safe in the beginning, but sending me a gift meant they knew my address. They quickly wormed their way into my life and started trying to plan it for me. It was all "dangling carrots" sort of control– every time they learned about something I needed or wanted to do, they would say they could help me get or do it and then start manipulating me with all their offers of presents and "help." Before I knew it, I was caught up in a big plan that included them driving out to where I lived, throwing all my stuff into a moving van, and taking me to live with them and their spouse (of whom they spoke in a very disparaging and infantilizing manner and whom they also clearly manipulated and controlled).

They had high demands of my time and energy. They wanted me to video Skype with them for hours every day. I protested because it was taking up all my time and energy and leaving nothing for me. I couldn't get housework done, I couldn't write, I couldn't just rest and stare at the wall (a favorite pastime of mine, similar to running a defrag program on a hard drive). I became frazzled and stressed. They wouldn't take no for an answer. They grew more and more demanding. Just as I was about to pull away from them, they started saying they thought they might be Autistic, too. They wanted my help and advice. They pulled me back in with that, as it's so difficult for me to say no to someone who needs my help. Their demands got larger: I was going to move in with them and go into business with them. I could see that they wanted me because a diagnosed Autistic person would add an air of legitimacy to their business. They were using me as an object, not treating me as a human being. I began to panic as they talked about leaving my car behind, ignoring my complaints that it would leave me stranded and helpless. "That's silly. You can drive my car whenever you need to," was the response. It did not comfort me. Loss of control over my life and being trapped or stuck someplace are among my biggest fears.

It all came to a head when my electricity got shut off temporarily due to a clerical error and a lost payment. I was relaxing in the dark, waiting, because there was nothing I could do about the electricity until morning. I was stressed nearly to my limits. I was naked because my apartment had grown stifling with no electricity to run the fans. There was a knock at the door and I ignored it, as I always do when I'm not expecting anyone. Then a voice in the hallway announced themselves as a police officer and I froze in fear. Some of my past abuses have been at the hands of police officers with scanty understanding of autism.

I could hear the police in the hall, talking to neighbors. I couldn't hear everything that was said, but I heard one neighbor say that he knew I was in there. Whatever was said, it made the police worried enough to break down my door– it turned out that my predator had gotten frustrated at not being able to reach me for a Skype visit and sent the police to my door for a welfare check as punishment for avoiding them. I don't want to go into all the results of that welfare check, but I will leave you to just imagine how it went. How would you expect the police to respond when sent to an apartment by a frantic sounding person telling all sorts of wild tales? What would you expect their response to be when they knocked, heard movement, broke the door, and found a naked person, incapable of speech, sitting in the darkness in an apartment with no utilities? It did not go well. There were repercussions that took months to work through, but the experience gave me the courage to break off the interactions with my predator.

I was fortunate that the victimization never went past the level of emotional manipulation, but if they had swooped me up and moved me to their home, who knows what would have happened once I was isolated and under their control? And "swoop" is the right word here– the entire "relationship" went from innocent-seeming gift to police breaking down my door in less than two weeks. It all moved so fast and was so overwhelming. I was always several steps behind in understanding what was happening. They took advantage of my Autistic traits and used them against me to corral me into a completely untenable position.

I am middle-aged and very experienced, yet someone was still able to figure out where the chinks were in my armor, insinuating their way into my life in an abusive manner. And they did all this from a distance. They renewed my sense of vulnerability and increased my fear of letting new people into my life. It was so easy for them to take my life by storm that way. How much more vulnerable are people half my age? How much more vulnerable are children? Who is looking out for us? Who can we trust?

Autism acceptance means presuming competence, but it also means building a community that helps Autistic people defend ourselves against predators. The standard education children get about "stranger danger" is not enough. So many times, the predator is not a stranger, or they are very skilled at convincing their target that they are not really a stranger. Predators try to overwhelm us by moving things along fast. Autistic people need to know that it's okay to slow down, to take our time, to think things through. People who demand instant answers and instant actions from us should be questioned. If they are truly on our side, they will accept a slow response. Demanding that we keep up their fast pace is a "red flag" that can help warn us that a person might not have our best interests at heart.

We need to learn how to locate mentors in the community who we can turn to for sound advice. A mentor could be a parent, a teacher, a trusted therapist, a friend– anyone who has a proven track record of helping us to make decisions that are good for us and come from our own choices. If a new person comes into your life and wants your address, your phone number, wants to make grand plans to uproot your life, wants to push you to a more intimate friendship than you are ready for– anything that makes you uncomfortable– it is good to be able to talk it through with a mentor. It can be a dangerous world and we Autistics are vulnerable. There are people who know that and seek us out to use, exploit, manipulate, and worse. We need to be careful and autism acceptance recognizes the risks while working to protect our autonomy and dignity. A person can be competent yet operating under incomplete information.

Presume competence, but help us steer a safe course when we ask for advice. Help us steer our own course– don't choose for us. But please help us see the potential obstacles and learn how to avoid them. The world can be a scary place for anyone and we are especially vulnerable to violence and victimization. Those of us who are very articulate or possessed of a precocious intellect are particularly at risk because too often our sense of judgment about people is not at the same level as our vocabulary. Our academic achievements can mask our social vulnerability, leading others to neglect giving us the help we need to avoid victimization. Be extra careful to help those of us who might seem least vulnerable because sometimes they are the most vulnerable of all.

W is for Women

Autistic women are rebels. In a world where autism is nearly always spoken of as a "childhood disease" and the alleged 1:4 ratio of female:male ends up being interpreted as if female Autistics don't even exist, or are so passingly rare that one shouldn't even bother looking for evidence of us, just existing as an Autistic woman is a radical act.

We are seeing more and more awareness of adult, female Autistics, but as with other aspects of autism, awareness is not always helpful and does not often lead to acceptance. What I usually see is an attempt to define "the female Autistic" as if we are a single, monolithic type. We are not. Some of us go barefaced; some have huge make-up collections. Some of us are math and science mavens; some are poets and musicians. (Some are both at once.) Some of us are cis, some are trans, some identify as female but not woman, some would prefer being called anything *but* female, and so on in every combination of gender or genderlessness imaginable. The same with sexuality: some are asexual, some aromantic, some lesbian, some heterosexual, some bisexual or pansexual, some monogamous, some polyamorous, some ... well, we could do this all day.

The short version is that there is no one way to be an Autistic woman. Or an Autistic female. There are many words for my gender, including metagender, igender, genderqueer, genderfuid, gendervague (a term specifically coined to describe the way being Autistic influences our gender identities), but the word that best captures my own gender is "epicene." I am not personally involved with The Order of the Epicene but I applaud their concise definition of the gender identity: "that which exhibits characteristics of both genders, yet is neither."[92] As an epicene, I prefer to have no second-person pronouns, using my name instead of "he" or "she." Having no second-person pronouns can make for clumsy writing, however, so I also accept the 'singular they' as a respectful way to refer to me. Some turn their grammar-loving nose up at the singular they, but it has a long history in classic literature.[93] Those of us who choose 'they' as our preferred personal pronouns are taking acceptable grammar only one step farther.

I identify as both female and male (and neither) but not as woman or man. I carry elements of both in my presentation and sometimes present myself more as female, sometimes more as male. I'm not "going through a phase" and I take my gender identity so seriously that I am planning reconstructive surgery to claim and shape my body in ways that will make me more comfortable and less agitated. The body I live in causes me daily anxiety, bursts of anger, and much preventable suffering. I share this with you, gentle reader, to help you understand the importance of taking gender identity seriously, whether it is your own, your child's, or anyone's. There is no such thing as too young or too old to understand one's gender or decide to transition. Moreover, autism should never be considered a reason to deny someone the support and relief of recognizing and respecting their expression of gender or non-gender.

---

92. http://epiceneorder.org/en/
93. http://www.pemberley.com/janeinfo/austheir.html

Like many other chapters, this one landed on W but the ideas contained within span the entire alphabet. And even though W is for Women, this is a great opportunity to look at gender issues for all genders (and ungenders), not just one. I am a strong believer in gender non-binarism, but I might slip up here. I've spent decades steeped in the dominant culture and am still working on shedding my unthinking wording and concepts. If I say something erasing or excluding, I hope you can forgive me as I work to be ever more understanding and ever more inclusive.

Our great diversity as Autistic females/women doesn't stop people from trying to define the female Autistic experience. I have read books or entered groups that were very alienating for me because one way of being Autistic was held up as "the way Autistic women are" and fitting into that definition would have been procrustean for me– requiring my cutting off parts of myself to squeeze into the narrow little definition. When so many Autistic women talk about feeling like aliens among other women, it is a shame when we end up feeling like aliens among other Autistic women as well. We can be a sisterhood without being identical twins. The ways we are related run deeper than blood, and so often deeper than surface similarities as well.

This summer, I met an Autistic woman who feels more like a sister to me than my flesh-and-blood sister does. On the surface, we are different in so many ways. She has children; I don't. She is successful in a career (although she admitted that she holds it together with much more struggle than most people see); I live on disability because I have never been able to keep a job. She has lovely taste in clothes, flowing hair, and a mainstream "feminine" beauty; I am beautiful, too, but I keep my hair a couple of inches long and wear the same t-shirt for days in a row– not so stereotypically feminine.   We are very different females who probably would never have met if it weren't for the autism connection.

But from the first moment, I knew I had met kin. And she later said it felt the same for her. There is something about being an Autistic woman that runs too deep to be distracted by the superficial ways we tend to categorize either women or Autistics. It's deeper than ideas of femme/butch, more important than worldly success or the apparent lack thereof. That connection among Autistic women runs deeper, even, than the chromosomes. Recently, another friend came out as trans, and I already knew months before. I had spotted a sister in her long before she announced what her proper pronouns are. There wasn't a moment of surprise, merely confirmation, because I had already *seen* her at least a year before.[94] Sisters know our own.

I know this all sounds mysterious and esoteric. It's not the kind of thing that makes for a good checklist in the appendix of a book about What It Means to Be an Autistic Female. I never found much value in those checklists anyway. They always read to me as wide nets set to catch everyone, with multiple entries that read like: "she is extremely X or else she is not one little bit X at all," and, "she either really loves Y or has no interest in Y at all." What kind of checklist is that? It's about as useful as making a checklist to determine if an organism is alive and putting entries like, "it moves around a whole lot or else it is rooted in one place."

So then, what can I say about Autistic women? I can say that we're grossly underdiagnosed, partly because of messed up checklists that try to paint a reductionist portrait of a group of humans who cannot be reduced to a simple list. This is a problem for many Autistics, but underdiagnosis is particularly rampant among females and other marginalized groups. I can say that our needs have not begun to be met and won't be until others work harder to understand us, difficult though that can be. Much of what we need is the same as what all Autistics need: at root, a recognition of our value, independent of our perceived productivity; accommodations that do not begrudge us our needs; acceptance of who we are, not hopes of molding us into someone who moves, speaks, and thinks differently (and, thus, is not us but rather some different, imagined person).

We have some differences. We have an overlapping but different set of

---

94. **Editor's note:** Hi! Yeah, that was me. No need for guessing games. If you want to read my coming out novels, they are *Defiant* and the first book of the Mirror Project trilogy, and they were written simultaneously. – Monje

safety needs compared to male Autistics, for example. This is because, generally speaking, the dangerous situations we encounter are different, mainly because society at large treats perceived-male and perceived-female people so differently. We live in a world where males are encouraged to be the sexual pursuers and females are encouraged to be the sexual gatekeepers. Both these roles, artificial as they are in the first place, are complicated by the boundary-destroying ways so many Autistic people are treated. We are often infantilized, leading to a sense of helplessness that manifests in being unsure how to pursue, or how to know if one is being pursued, or how to know if one's pursuit is welcome, or how to keep a pursuer at bay safely and with kindness. These are difficulties for all people who have experienced multiple boundary transgressions in childhood and these struggles are complicated by society's gender views being laid on top of everything. The fight to learn boundaries is genderless; gender and gender roles bring out many differences in how these boundary struggles play out. And as if all this "battle of the sexes" garbage weren't frustrating and dangerous enough as it is, those Autistics who struggle to have their true gender acknowledged and respected face some of the worst oppression and danger of us all.

Being infantilized and denied a chance to learn strong boundaries is a risk all disabled children face. Autistic children face an extra barrier when they are subjected to compliance training. Compliance training intentionally works toward breaking a person down and rebuilding them in a different image. Compliance training teaches a person that what someone else wants is more important than what the person wants for themselves. Compliance training teaches that resistance is futile and torment ends more quickly when a person just gives in and does what others want.

Children raised with compliance training struggle to find a sense of self in the midst of all the demands placed on them. And children raised with compliance training learn early on that they do not own their body. They often learn that they do not even own their will. Now, add in society's demands on men and women and you can see the troubles that Autistic people of all genders and ungenders often face. How can a person who has never been taught what good boundaries look like, who's never had a chance to learn what it means to have one's will acknowledged and respected, be expected to learn how to cope with unwanted demands and expectations, except by yielding pliantly while taking their emotions and mind to some hidden place to preserve them?

Those statistics you saw in the last chapter about rape and abuse? They apply to all Autistics, but Autistics viewed as female take the lion's share of that rape and abuse. There are counters that we try to teach our non-autistic daughters: run away, scream, kick, hit, bite, shout "NO!" as loudly as you can. Every one of those defense mechanisms have been systematically disabled in girls who go through compliance training under any name or overarching philosophy. Compliance training, by design, creates victims out of Autistic men and compliance training coupled with social standards creates victims out of Autistic women.

It is terrible when the defining factors Autistic women share are things like oppression, lack of services, lack of recognition, and widespread abuse. That is why I love to focus on the sisterhood we share. I prefer to think about the bonding moments. I met an Autistic girl recently and was pleasantly shocked to see how much easier it is for me to make eye contact with her than with most people. She doesn't speak, but she reached out to touch my face, then laid her head against me, and I felt myself melt from the inside out with shared love. This is how I define my life as an Autistic female.

I am one of those I mentioned above who identifies as female but struggles with the notion of being a woman. When I try to see what it is about me that is female, I can look to myself and see it. When I try to see what it is about me that is "woman," I can only look to others and attempt definition by seeing where I fit into the larger group of those who are women. When comparing myself to all women, I feel lost and alien. When comparing myself to Autistic women, I feel some sense of belonging. True, we are very different. But so much of those differences are superficial things that don't matter when it comes to finding real connection with others. I am not like my sisters; I am part of a deep connection of sisterhood we share.

I can't really tell you what it means to be an Autistic woman. I am only one female among so many. But I can ask you to be patient with us, to listen to our stories and piece together a patchwork understanding of who we are as a group. Most importantly, to take each of us as an individual. We are each, perhaps, representative of the larger group, but you cannot treat Autistic women as a monolithic entity any more than you can treat any category of people that way. Cherish our "yes" and respect our "no." In fact, I would like you to value our "no" highest of all because this is the response that, so often, we have won with blood and tears and so much struggle. If you want to respect, assist, and love us best, remember above all else that an Autistic "no" is a sacred and inviolate thing.

X is for X Factor

You've heard of the show, *X Factor*? In case you haven't, it's a television talent show where people compete for a prize. The goal of the show is to decide who has "the X factor," which is defined as, "a noteworthy special talent or quality." There is an aura of mystery surrounding the X factor–what is it? Where does it come from? It is portrayed as a near-mystical trait that can be fostered in some but is absent in others.

Autism has an X factor – several, in fact – surrounding it and it's time to talk about how the myths of autism X factors work against autism acceptance.

I have noticed two main categories of X factors surrounding autism: spiritual and savant. We talked about "savant syndrome" back in Chapter S, but there is more to say about the savant X factors of autism. People are fascinated by outliers: Bobby Fischer, Albert Einstein, John McEnroe, Jesse Owens, Admiral Grace Hopper. In the world of autism, we have famous outliers as well: the great livestock facility designer Temple Grandin, the great rock instrument engineer John Elder Robison, the great artist Stephen Wiltshire, the Nobel Prize-winning economist Vernon L. Smith, to name a few.

If you are a chess player, no one honestly expects you to be as great as Bobby Fischer. If you major in physics, you won't be told every day that you should be more successful than you are because Einstein was so successful. Taking up tennis won't have people judging you by how you compare to McEnroe and you won't be considered a failure at running if you are only half as fast as Jesse Owens. Women are often held to unrealistic standards, but no one tells women they aren't living up to their potential because they haven't achieved what Admiral Hopper did.

I can't tell you how many times my struggles in graduate school were dismissed by people who said, "have you heard of Temple Grandin?" though. Umm ... of course I've heard of Temple Grandin. She's probably the most famous Autistic person in the world and I'm Autistic, so yes. I have, indeed, heard of Temple Grandin. But as soon as I hear that question, my best option is to walk away from the conversation right there because I know what comes next: a pep talk about how Temple Grandin is successful and that means I can be, too. There are very few common denominators between Dr. Grandin and myself. We are both female. We are both Autistic. We both love animals. That's about it. People don't seem to realize that comparing me to Dr. Grandin and expecting me to achieve what she has achieved just because we are both Autistic is not so different from me going into any restaurant with a female chef and asking her why she is not wealthy and famous like Julia Child because both are female and both love to cook for a living. Why does the chef at the lovely little bistro down the street not have book contracts? Why has Dan Aykroyd not done comedy sketches honoring her fame by mocking her quirks? Why is there no movie about her life?

If I knew the chef from the bistro and she were complaining to me about not being able to make ends meet because she feels she deserves a raise but hasn't gotten one in years, would it be helpful for me to shame her by comparing her achievements to those of Julia Child? Of course not. Why is it then that people don't realize that's what they're doing when I complain about dropping out of graduate school because I was unable to get the necessary accommodations to finish my degree and they respond by telling me how great Temple Grandin is?

I should note that I am not intending to diminish or degrade Dr. Grandin for her achievements. She has worked hard to get to where she is. She had a lot of help to get there, but she also had a lot of determination and brilliance and innate talent. The world is a better place because Temple Grandin has been in it, but it is just as wrong to use her as a signpost of some autism X factor that we all should share as it is to assume that all Black men could run like Jesse Owens if they really tried, or that all white women could be Cindy Crawford if they just went on the right diet and applied their makeup just so. There isn't some mystical X factor that makes all Autistic people able to achieve the things that our famous outliers have achieved, and it is humiliating and dismissive to compare us to famous high-achievers just because we are both Autistic. I draw a little- don't dismiss my talent because I can't draw like Stephen Wiltshire unless your aim is to shame and frustrate me out of wanting to draw at all. If I can only be a good artist if I am as good as one of the best artists, why should I even bother trying? If I failed to earn my doctorate because I was denied the accommodation of doing my teaching hours in an online asynchronous classroom to accommodate my circadian rhythm disorder, how will I feel encouraged when your response to my pain is to give me a pep talk that consists of "You can do it; Temple Grandin did it!" Did Dr. Grandin have a circadian rhythm disorder? Was she living far below the poverty threshhold when she went to graduate school? To compare us so blithely dismisses the very real barriers I face. Dr. Grandin faced barriers, too- some similar to mine and some very different – but our lives are not identical and it is shaming and dismissive to respond to my failure by pointing out that someone else succeeded.

Another autism X factor statement I periodically hear that makes me cringe is that "autistic people are the next step in human evolution." Related to this is Temple Grandin's assertion that, were autism not in the gene pool, humanity would consist only of "a bunch of people standing around in a cave, chatting and socializing and not getting anything done." Dr. Hans Asperger has been quoted as saying that "it seems that for success in science or art a dash of autism is essential." These are all X factor quotes, too. These are quotes that teach us to value Autistic people because of a belief that Autistic people are superior– either overall or within certain spheres of human achievement. What is not always immediately apparent is that this attitude of elevating autism as something that conveys superhuman powers is just as "othering" as depicting autism as a tragic lack of genuine humanity. It might seem to be better to portray us as possessing an X factor not belonging to non-autistic people and, indeed, many people relish these sorts of elevating statements, mistaking them as the pinnacle of autism acceptance. They are quite the opposite.

Now, I should interrupt here to say that if you are not autistic and you hear an Autistic person saying these sorts of things, it is not your place to take them to task. If a member of a marginalized group is othering themselves this way, let them be. We will work out these sorts of issues among ourselves and you will not come across well at all if you try to tell Autistic people how to view ourselves or refer to ourselves. Just as was mentioned in Chapter I: If someone chooses to call themselves a "person with autism" that is their choice and you must respect the autonomy of self-identification. We each have the right to self-identify as we choose and have that identity respected by others. If an Autistic person tells you, a non-autistic person, that they are the next step in human evolution, let them be. Maybe they really need that identity at the moment. But if you are a non-autistic person writing or speaking about Autistic people, please avoid these X factor statements that only serve to distance us from the rest of humanity. When we are held forth as something different or higher than other humans, it makes it harder for us to get the accommodations we need in order to get through our daily lives, thrive, and succeed with our strengths. When you promote our value based on outliers who are really good with math, science, design, music, art, and other human accomplishments, you teach people to value us based on what outstanding accomplishments we can contribute to humankind rather than emphasizing our inherent worth as human beings.

Non-autistic people get to be considered worthy and valuable simply because they are living human beings. Do we not deserve the same? When people are valued only for what they can contribute to others, we are all constantly held on trial to prove our right to continue to exist in society. Value us because we are, because we exist, because we are your fellow human beings, not because you think that keeping us alive means one of us will discover the cure for cancer.

The other X factor– the spiritual X factor– is just as othering and just as frustrating. You've heard those statements before? "Autistic people are so much more spiritual."

"Autistic people are directly in touch with God."

"Autistic people are here to teach us lessons, to lead us down a path of discovery, to raise the vibrations of the world's energy."

"Autistic people are Indigo Children and Crystal Spirits."

"Autistic people are so much more highly evolved spiritually."

First, you should realize that these kinds of statements are very erasing to Autistic atheists. A University of Boston study among Autistics who use online social media found 26% of Autistic participants were atheists; compare this to a 16% rate of atheism among a similar demographic sample of the general population. This means that X factor statements about some "spiritual" quality of Autistic people are automatically dismissing thousands of Autistic people who would be uncomfortable, at best, at being described as some kind of spiritual messiah or Indigo Child.

Before you jump on that Indigo bandwagon, by the way, you should know that Jenny McCarthy, known now for being very vocal in her support for the soundly debunked "vaccines cause autism" theory, began her public autism journey by claiming that she is an "Indigo" and her Autistic son is a "Crystal." I just thought you might like to know the company you will be keeping if you decide to saddle Autistic people with the Indigo autism X factor. It is no coincidence that McCarthy moved from a New Age explanation of her son to a "vaccine-induced injury" explanation. The New Age Indigo movement and the anti-vaccine movement are close bedfellows, linked through a mistrust of mainstream science.

Wait, you've never heard of Indigo people or Crystals? It's something that comes out of New Age thought and has become very popular in certain groups of people who like to say that Autistics, people with ADHD, and people with learning disabilities are Indigo or Crystal children. The idea originated in the 1970s but grew in popularity during the late 1990s, most likely due to parents who were disappointed after ending up with neurodivergent children and looking for an X factor to soothe that disappointment, to "prove" that their child is even better than the neurotypical child they wanted and are grieving about not having. The list of traits for determining if someone is an Indigo or Crystal cast such a wide net, they produce the Forer Effect– that is to say, they can be applied to pretty much anyone. Being a "Crystal" is sometimes synonymous with being an "Indigo," but more often I see Crystals mentioned as being more "highly evolved" than Indigos. In the case of Jenny McCarthy, she claimed that her role as an Indigo was to clear away specific "energies" to make room for her son's "Crystal energy" to work. Writings about Autistic children as "Crystals" emphasize things like psychic abilities, and they re-frame things like sensory issues and meltdowns as evidence of mystical powers. If you read a bit about Indigo Children, you will find people claiming that they are the "next stage in human evolution." Hmmm... where have we heard that phrase before?

What you believe is what you believe, but please think carefully before laying these "burdens of specialness" on Autistic people. This is not autism acceptance– it is making Autistic people into a curiosity, setting us apart with "otherness" whether it is intellectual or spiritual. Rather than increasing autism acceptance, it sets up unrealistic expectations that are dehumanizing and that decrease our ability to get the assistance and accommodations we need. Why should anyone wish to accommodate us if we are all so elevated, so above the rest of humankind, so destined to be the next Einsteins or Prophets of the New Aeon? We each have our own personal pattern of strengths and weaknesses. Work with our individual needs. Value us for the individual human beings we are, not for some X factor myth of superiority we possess, either collectively or as manifest in our outliers. If we are valued because some of us can produce amazing works of art and science, what does that mean for those of us who are not producing anything society values? Can we get our needs met or are we simply the social cost of producing a few, rare geniuses? Valuing us only for the work of a tiny handful has the unintentional consequence of relegating the rest of us to the status of ballast. History has already shown us the danger of viewing disabled people this way.

Y is for Yesterday

"The past is never dead. It's not even past." – William Faulkner[95]

Something that doesn't get mentioned as often as other autistic traits is our memories. We seem to make stronger memories than non-autistic people, and we hold memories longer. Most Autistics I have talked to have more intensely cemented and more prolific early childhood memories than our non-autistic peers. And it seems that many Autistic adults have PTSD from growing up Autistic– whether identified or unrealized– in a world that is not always very friendly to people like us. In fact, our traumatic memories affect us so deeply that I have long suspected that many of the traits currently considered signs of autism (for example, affect dysregulation) are actually signs of the PTSD so many Autistic people live with. I suspect that autism would look a bit different in a world where we were accepted for who we are, a world where we were protected and nurtured instead of bullied and victimized.

PTSD is caused by a nervous system reaction to traumatic experiences – type I trauma: one very intense experience; or type II trauma: an ongoing series of traumatic experiences that might be intense but that can do just as much damage at a significantly lower intensity if there are enough of them, ongoing for long enough. Like drops of water wearing through stone, a

---

95. Requiem for a Nun.

series of smaller traumas can eat away at a person's nervous system when they are perceived as threats against which the individual is helpless. Some examples of this steady erosion leading to PTSD are being stuck in school every day with bullies, abuse in the home, damaging therapies that focus only on changing behaviors with no connection to the inner life and needs of the Autistic person, and regular exposure to intense sensory input (bearing in mind that "intense" for someone with an Autistic nervous system and sensory processing might seem "peaceful" to someone with a more neurotypical nervous system).

An Autistic person who is regularly subjected to trauma– whether from bullying and abuse or from sensory onslaught that can be caused by external stimuli or the unexpected internal stimulus of strong emotions that may be unanticipated due to alexithymia[96]– ends up spending their life steeped in ongoing and unpredictable stress and anxiety that can lead to semi-permanent or permanent neurological damage over time. In the last decade or so, an association has been found between trauma and the diagnosis of borderline personality disorder (BPD). Some researchers are considering whether Complex Post-Traumatic Stress Disorder (C-PTSD) and BPD are actually the same thing. And BPD is a common misdiagnosis Autistic people are given before they are accurately identified as Autistic– especially female Autistics. This is all illustrative of the complicated tangle of autism, trauma, stress, and anxiety.

The traumas that arise from being misunderstood, from being bullied, from coping with daily sensory onslaught, from harsh compliance training ... the damage caused by going through every day bathed in stress hormones ... the ways trauma affect all brains, let alone Autistic brains ... these topics could fill an entire book– or several– and there are others far more qualified to write those books than I am. My task here is to put this topic into the context of autism acceptance. What do you, as an Autistic person, or as someone who loves someone Autistic, or as someone who serves the needs of Autistic people, or just as a caring human being who has decided to learn

---

96. Difficulty in recognizing and identifying emotions, something estimated to be part of the Autistic experience for as many as 40% to 65% of us, compared to an estimated 10% rate in the general population.

more about Autistic people and autism acceptance without actually knowing any Autistic people yet,[97] what do you need to know about how our terrific memories are maybe not so terrific when it comes to a lifelong build-up of stress and pain?

The bottom line is this: Don't take a hard attitude toward us. Don't call us oversensitive– we have precisely the amount of sensitivity we have and you must not judge us for that. Every single one of us, even that Autistic person who seems to have had a charmed life with good employment and a satisfying social life, have been through and are going through things you cannot see, things science is still learning to quantify. When you touch an Autistic child on the hand or hair and they let out a scream and struggle against you, your job in that moment is to back off and remain calm. When an Autistic adult becomes anxious and shaky because you re-painted your waiting room a cheery yellow, your job in that moment is to help them get to a safe place where they can calm down and process the change.

Autistic people are not "engaging in bad behaviors" when we get triggered by things that seem insignificant to you. We are not being oversensitive. We are not "choosing to be upset" by something. I'm not going to tell you that we're complete angels who never have a selfish or cruel moment. Of course that's not true. We're human beings with imperfections just like everyone. But we are not "faking distress in order to manipulate" you as I have more than once seen a non-autistic person claim about an Autistic person's very real breakdown.

You may not understand our triggers. What upsets an Autistic person may seem trivial or you may not even be able to figure out what set one of us off (although I hope you will try to understand if you can). Sometimes even we are not sure what is upsetting us. But I assure you, the distress is anything but trivial to us, and it is damaging in the long term. Those stress hormones that damage everyone, Autistic or not, when we are regularly subjected to them every day, for years and years? Those are the same stress hormones that flood through our system when we are re-traumatized by stressful triggers in our daily life, whether new sensory assaults or things that flood us with

---

97. Or, perhaps, without realizing that you know any of us. We are pretty obvious once you know what you're looking for, but we still seem to be mysteriously invisible to most people.

overwhelming memories of older abuses and victimizations we have survived.

For people who have been traumatized, the past is not dead. As Faulkner reminds us, it is not even past. We live and re-live our traumas. What can you do for us? If you know something is upsetting to us, help us to avoid it. You are not coddling us; you are protecting us. It is not cowardly and avoidant; it is healthy. We need to feel calm and safe in order to heal from past traumas. We need to know we can trust you. We need help avoiding or coping with those people we can't trust.

We need help getting around the unavoidable people who trigger us, whether unconsciously or actively and with delight: the landlord with the loud voice who talks over us and treats us like a child; the neighborhood bullies who intentionally gun their race car engines or park right outside with windows down and stereo blasting because they think it's funny to send an Autistic adult into a screaming meltdown; the dentist who shames his Autistic patient for reacting badly to dental work, perhaps not realizing that researchers have found that certain groups of people do not respond as well biologically to dental anesthesia, including people with red hair and Autistic people; the classmate who delights in picking on an Autistic student to the point of emotional explosion; the parent who constantly misjudges the motives of their Autistic child and punishes her for things beyond her ability to control.

Life is filled with stress-inducing people. I don't have to convince you of this fact, because if you are reading these words you already know it. It doesn't matter what your neurology or position in life is. You already know that your life– everybody's life– includes people who are very difficult to cope with. But don't let that universal reality prevent you from understanding the very real damage that this kind of stress can do to a nervous system that has already been through a life filled with stress and trauma. You might not understand the trauma because so much of it is internal and because you don't see the impact of seemingly small things in another person's life, but I hope you can understand and accept that signs of trauma are real and need to be addressed.

Respect our need for calm and comfort. Some of us have very damaged nervous systems and we are not being weak when we ask for relief from the stress. We are being very strong in advocating for deep needs. You are not indulging us or rewarding us when you help us to maintain a calm and soothing environment. You are showing compassion and respect when you help us to feel safe and have the space to self-heal.

If you catch yourself thinking or saying things like, "you just have to get used to that," or "the world isn't going to give you a free pass on this," or "just buck up and deal with it," stop yourself and remember how much we are already dealing with. Many of us are carrying years of deep wounds and we just need a break. We need to have a place we feel safe. We need to have a person we can trust. Don't take those things away from us out of some misguided belief that you will toughen us up or make us stronger by forcing us to face adversity. If you think we are weak, consider the possibility that you think that because you are seeing the end result of years of being crushed by traumas. Everyone has their breaking point. Do not judge others who break in ways or under pressures you do not understand.

If you are interacting with an Autistic person and you see defensiveness rising, don't push. Slow down. Respect the underlying traumas you may not be able to see. Stay calm, centered, and compassionate. Let the Autistic person set the speed. Give them space to feel more in control of themselves and, if possible, more in control of the situation. If you can help us learn to cope better, most of us would welcome that, but don't try to teach coping skills in the heat of the moment. No one learns well when they are in the middle of a stress reaction. Wait until a calm time to talk about ways to cope with stress.

None of this is easy. When I begin to get distressed, most people get distressed along with me. I deeply value those people who are able to remain calm and help me to calm down. I know it's not easy. It's even harder when two Autistic people are having a conflict, because things often spiral out of control with the speed of a firestorm sweeping through a forest. I've lost friendships and communities in the middle of a mass meltdown affecting more than one Autistic person simultaneously. I've watched others tear through their social circles, burning bridges the whole way.

I'm definitely not saying anyone should tolerate abuse from anyone else, and I'm not saying that one person's feelings and traumas trump another person's. We all have to figure out how to live among each other without doing too much extra damage to ourselves or others. But part of autism acceptance is accepting that our world is hard on everybody and harder on Autistics than it ought to be. The late nineteenth-century Scottish theologian, Ian Maclaren, said, "be pitiful for every man is fighting a hard battle." Take these words to heart and seek to give everyone the benefit of the doubt.

Some people focus on how hard it is for them to live with Autistic people. I hope those people can stop and realize how hard it is for Autistic people to live with them. Yes, many of us seem to have hair-triggers. Yes, we can seem to go from zero to meltdown in less than a second. We know this is hard on you and many of us carry heavy burdens of guilt and shame because we know how our traumas affect those around us. All we ask is that you stop from time to time to remember how very much harder living with these traumas is on us than it is on those who have to watch us struggle through them.

Z is for Zzzzzzzzz

As I am writing this, it is nine at night and I have not had breakfast yet. This is because I've only been awake a few hours. There are plenty of people with judgmental words about this kind of schedule, but I don't keep it out of preference, nor due to laziness. I don't even keep it at all, in fact. My sleep and wake are very loosely tethered to the clock, if at all. I have a neurological condition called hypernychthemeral syndrome but more commonly known as Non-24-Hour Sleep-Wake Syndrome or just Non-24 for short. My body is an orchestra and the conductor– the suprachiasmatic nucleus (SCN) of my brain– is not sure what score we are reading from.

The CDC has estimated that 50 to 70 million adult Americans (between 21% and 29%) have some kind of sleep-wake disorder. A British study found a 17% rate of sleep-wake disorders in developing nations. My own estimate, based on reading study reports in medical journals, is that Autistics are at least three times more likely to have a sleep-wake disorder than the general population. If my math is correct, that means that roughly 51% to 87% of Autistics are struggling to get our SCNs on the right page. That translates to something like 2/3 of us. That's a lot of lost and shifted sleep.

Don't blame us. We don't want to be strung-out and exhausted. We don't want to sleep through things we enjoy . . . Or even things we don't enjoy, really. We don't want to have to make our life choices while groggy or irritable from lack of sleep. We don't want to have to run triage on everything in our life to try to fit it all in around a sleep-wake life that doesn't want to fit anywhere. And just as the symptoms of our traumas often are misidentified as being part of our autism, symptoms of sleep-wake disorders get erroneously chalked up to autism, too. So much of what many people believe autism to be is really not autism at all, but related things so very many of us struggle with.

Where the blame can really get thick, though, is with the standard treatments for sleep-wake disorders. Most of the known successful treatments conflict with our neurology in one way or another. When we avoid those things that aren't working well for us (or are actively working against us) we risk getting blamed and judged as non-compliant or told we don't really care about getting up on time and are making up excuses to shirk responsibility. Please be aware that standard sleep treatments are impossible for many of us. If you are trying to help an Autistic person with their sleep, be gentle and listen to what they tell you. There is no point in pressuring us to tolerate extreme discomfort. What good is it doing us to use a sleep treatment that makes us completely miserable for most or all of our waking hours?

If you are Autistic and blaming yourself for not complying with sleep treatments, stop being so hard on yourself. So often, I see Autistics second-guessing ourselves and feeling guilt or shame at not being able to do things we have convinced ourselves we "ought" to be able to do (or others have pressured us into accepting their view that we aren't doing everything we could or should). I've done it plenty myself, telling myself I just didn't try hard enough or put up with distress long enough to see a difference. Being more gentle and understanding with myself is a work in progress. I encourage all my fellow Autistics to be gentle with themselves and not to succumb to the temptation to torture themselves in the name of living up to what others have suggested we "should" be able to do. Listen to your body. Respect your comfort levels. It's one thing to challenge yourself to grow and change in positive ways. I completely support that. But it is another thing entirely to grit your teeth and endure suffering because the alternative is shame and guilt. You are not weak, inferior, or lesser in any way if your body and nervous system protest at stimuli they are not equipped to handle.

Society helps us put unrealistic pressures on ourselves about things that just don't work for us. Melatonin, for example. Awareness of this hormone has spread and it's probably been recommended to you by friends, family, doctors, maybe even strangers. Melatonin can be very helpful, especially for mild sleep disturbances and disorders. But the hormone affects different people different ways. I can't take it, myself, because it quickly plunges me into a frighteningly deep depressive state. This isn't a typical reaction– many people find relief from depression through melatonin or a melatonin agonist drug, but enough people respond to melatonin with depression for it to be listed as an official potential side-effect. When I dug through the medical journals, I found that people who are already depressed or prone to depression are at higher risk of becoming depressed when taking melatonin. And, as discussed in Chapter D, several studies have indicated a much higher rate of depression and anxiety among us Autistic folks, so we need to be especially careful and pay attention to what our bodies tell us when we try to improve our sleep with melatonin.

Another common sleep treatment requires hours in front of a very bright therapy light. It's very common for Autistic people to perceive very bright light as a painful sensory assault. I can just barely tolerate it; for others it is impossible. In my case, I find I get better results when I sleep outdoors and am awakened naturally by sunlight. The sun, even on an overcast day, is much brighter than a therapy light but the light is spread out over the entire sky and much easier for me to tolerate, especially if I am camping and far away from all the reflective metal surfaces that surround me in a city. For me, a city is a horrible melange of sensory assaults. Sleeping outdoors gives my brain enough bright light and dark night to help the orchestral conductor in my SCN figure out what score we're playing. It's a little tune I like to call asleep by midnight and awake by nine a.m. That's not a sleep-wake schedule that will win me any awards in business or academia, but it's a lot more liveable for me than this free-running, untethered, unpredictable Non-24 I return to every time I start sleeping indoors again.[98]

Of course, I do realize that fixing my sleep disorder by living outdoors is a pretty extreme solution and not one that will work for . . . well, nearly anybody other than me and maybe Grizzly Adams or Bear Grylls. But it is a great illustration of just how hard it can be to figure out what to do with a brain that seems to be set for living on Mars instead of Earth. And it is a terrific example of just how distressing the standard sleep disorder treatments are to my nervous system when I prefer living outdoors to melatonin and therapy lamps.

People who don't have these extreme sleep difficulties seem to take sleep for granted and too often have little (or no) compassion for those of us who can't get our nervous system aligned with the cycles of the sun and the rotations of the clock hands. It's not as simple as going to Target to buy a really good alarm clock (as one luminary in the Autistic community suggested to me.) And the therapies that have been shown to work are really tough on people with very sensitive nervous systems.

Help us get better sleep if you can, but don't blame us if we aren't able to follow the usual prescription. Help us learn to fit our lives around our

---

98. Scientific American Mind article about my sleep disorder and how I treat it by sleeping outdoors: September/October 2015: Out of Sync by Emily Laber-Warren, pp. 31-9.

sleep in a way that works for us. Don't ridicule us for finding unusual ways to make our unusual lives work.[99] If you have a sleep-wake disorder yourself, don't punish yourself about it. You really are trying hard and it really is something you can't just fix with more discipline. Circadian rhythm disorders are not as well understood as we might like, so there isn't a lot of information available about how they affect people over the entire lifespan, but there are strong indicators that simply fighting a sleep-wake disorder, as opposed to finding a treatment that works for you can make it worse. In my own case, I had a severe time shift in my sleep-wake cycle[100] and when I fought against it to go to university at times that were the middle of my subjective night, it morphed into the Non-24 I live with today.

Rather than risk ending up in a similar situation, if you can't shift your sleep times without making yourself ill, consider shifting your goals. If you want to go to university, can distance education or night school work for you? If you were hoping to aim toward a career that realistically only happens in the daytime, for example, if you wanted to become a lawyer, is there a related field you might enjoy in which you would not have to spend the rest of your life fighting your brain's sleep and wake times? Just because you can fight it when you're young doesn't mean you will still be able to push your body that hard in middle age. And if, like me, pushing yourself that hard results in developing an even more severe and restricting sleep-wake disorder, you definitely would have been better off making more compatible career choices from the start, because rigid and unyielding Non-24 will put a halt to nearly any career you can imagine.

---

99. One example of an Autistic who makes circadian uncoupling work so well for her that she didn't even realize she had a sleep disorder is researcher Michelle Dawson. My own circadian struggles are far less fluid than hers. As in so many other areas of life, there is no one size fits all answer for Autistics. URL: http://autismcrisis.blogspot.com/2010/05/circadian-prison.html
100. Called Delayed Sleep Phase Disorder or DSPS

Conclusion

I mentioned that some people hear "autism acceptance" and think we are claiming that autism is nothing but "unicorns and rainbows." You've seen in the pages of this book that it is not. We have explored some serious and often intense topics. Autism acceptance is about seeing the beauty and living the joy of autism, but there are some very difficult aspects to the Autistic life – some inherent and many imposed on us from outside. Autism acceptance includes understanding our struggles and being compassionate toward us as we seek a better life for ourselves and others.

This is an amazing time for the Neurodiversity Movement in general and the Autistic Rights Movement specifically. There is so much we struggle against but our movements are blossoming, our numbers are growing, our communities are producing wonderful art, poetry, commentary, books, music, gatherings, and more. We stand on the threshold. There is hard work ahead of us but so much good awaits us. We are a vibrant community with a rich culture and whether you are Autistic yourself, the parent of one or more Autistic children (or Autistic adult children), dating or a friend to an Autistic person, a service provider of any type who interacts with Autistic people, or simply curious about Autistic culture and perceptions, you will want to explore Autistic culture.

Don't rely primarily on second-hand accounts– seek out the words of people who are actually Autistic themselves. Don't expect us to be all alike; we are not clones. But do notice our similarities because they definitely exist. As an Autistic who is part-time speaking and part-time unable to speak, I feel more kinship with Autistic people who do not speak at all than I do with non-Autistic people who speak full-time. Although demographic categories can be necessary for some discussions, try not to divide our community into types of people. If you insist on false dichotomies such as "high functioning" and "low functioning" you will come to us with so many preconceived notions that you will cheat yourself of true learning and connection.

Bring your open mind and seek to move beyond awareness to

understanding and true acceptance and you will find great treasure in venturing among us and knowing us as both individual human beings and as a culture. Approach with a willingness to learn and an open heart, and you will find yourself more welcomed than you could imagine.

◆　◆　◆

If you enjoyed this book, please read more books from Autonomous Press!

Also, please sign up to my newsletter for updates on my writing, music, art, and travels. Keep updated on my speaking engagements; ask questions and I will answer them in future newsletters, read reviews of books, websites, and movies; and much more. To sign up for the newsletter, visit my web page:

http://www.sparrowrose.com

Thank you for reading!

Sparrow
@SparrowRose
@UnstrangeMind

CPSIA information can be obtained
at www.ICGtesting.com
Printed in the USA
LVOW13s1611211216

518287LV00011B/1446/P